SHIFT

A SELF-LIBERATION HEALING PRACTICE:
MOVING FROM WOUNDED TO EMPOWERED

A Mind, Body, Energy, & Spirit Approach to Affirming
Your WHOLENESS

Mx. LENA QUEEN, LCSW, M.Ed.

Integrative Somatic Sex Therapist

Embodied Liberation Coach

SHIFT, A SELF-LIBERATION HEALING PRACTICE:
MOVING FROM WOUNDED TO EMPOWERED

A Mind, Body, Energy, & Spirit Approach to Affirming Your WHOLENESS

Published by EC Publishing

EC Publishing presents SHIFT, A SELF-LIBERATION
HEALING PRACTICE:
MOVING FROM WOUNDED TO EMPOWERED
A Mind, Body, Energy, & Spirit Approach to Affirming Your
WHOLENESS

Text © Talena "Lena" Queen, LCSW, M.Ed.

The moral rights of the author have been asserted.

Printed in the United States of America

Cover Design: Talena Queen

Illustrations:

Lotus Flower by Talena Queen, LCSW, M.Ed.

 via Canva

SHIFT, A Self-Liberation Infographic by

 Talena "Lena" Queen, LCSW, M.Ed. via Canva

The SHIFT Energy Center Chart by

Talena "Lena" Queen, LCSW, M.Ed. via Canva

Trade Paper ISBN: 978-1-7364800-0-7

E-Book ISBN: 978-1-7364800-2-1

ACKNOWLEDGMENT

To The Divine- Thank you for opening doorways, unclogging obstacles, and for your constant protection. Thank you for the blessings of peace, prosperity, protection, and pleasure with ease and without penalty from energy that is infinite and unobstructedly flowing.

To my Ancestors, Spirits, Guardians, and Guides- Thank you for leading me, trusting me and supporting my healing journey.

To Drea, Ronika, Mina, Makkah, & Charli-Thank you for your kinship and being community.

This is also for all the Black Girls, cis and trans, who have considered suicide when the rainbow is enuf &... to honor those who completed it. No matter our commitment to wholeness. We are choosing ourselves.

DEDICATION

To my daughter, Talena- the artist, furniture maker, self-liberator, amazing mother, my best friend and our family's chain breaker. Thank you for choosing me to be your mom and trusting me to rise to the occasion. To Bernard, my son-in-law, thank you for being you and being Talena's biggest fan and her earthly protector.

To my Kadee, Ororo, & Leo- thank you for loving your Nonee and being so happy that I am happy.

This is for our generational healing and is dedicated to you all.

TABLE OF CONTENTS

Opening

Introduction

Chapter 1

    Healing is Liberated Living   27

Chapter 2

    Healing 101: Becoming Healing-Centered   32

Chapter 3

    The Healing Power of Self-Compassion   39

Chapter 4

    From Wounded to Empowered: 46
        Becoming Unstuck

Chapter 5

    Healing Your Core Wounds: Honoring   54
    Vulnerability & Creating a Thriving Mindset

Chapter 6

    Embodied Intelligence: Activating Your   67
    Internal Resources of WHOLENESS

Chapter 7

    Developing a Presence Practice: 84
    Becoming a Self-Liberator

Chapter 8

    SHIFT, A Self-Liberation Practice   134

Resources

SHIFT Liberated Living Structure & Strategies   172

This page was left intentionally blank.

INTRODUCTION

Allow me to share a story with you.

ne afternoon while watching Disney's CoCo for the umpteenth time, myself laying on the couch as my daughter and granddaughter are laying on the floor in front of me (46yo)- my granddaughter, 5 years old, popped up and said, "Nonee, are you a Black girl?" I smiled and said, "Yes, I am a Black girl." She then turned to her mommy (26yo) and said, "Mommy, are you a

Black girl?". Her mom smiled and softly laughed, "Yes, Kadee, mommy's a Black girl. Kadee then gets up, and taps me on the nose and sings "You're a Black girl" then singing again while tapping her mother's nose "You're a Black girl" and then with a huge smile taps herself on the nose and says "I'mma a Black girl". My heart just swelled with joy. Her mother and I looked at each other knowingly. That, Beautiful Humans, is when you knew our healing work surrounding (and to dissolve) the harmful messages that Black girls internalize as self-limiting beliefs about our worth was taking hold, not just individually, but generationally. My granddaughter, my daughter, and myself understand our worth. This took place in early spring 2020. The story is an excerpt from an article I wrote called *Joy in My Blackness*.

Fast forward to today, there have been so many of life's ebbs and flows; however, this moment anchors us with gifts called presence and connection that anchor us to our truth- **YOU ARE WORTHY.** Worthy of what...*To live both pleasurably AND WHOLE.* At that moment, what we desired was our healing; healing deep, authentic, and lasting. Healing cleansed our wounds, protected our mind and body, and replenished our energy. Today, at 52, I and my daughter (32) have created empowered embodiments that allow us to experience safety and security within our relationship to ourselves and the courage to curate the relationships we want with each other and with those we wish to be in relationship. Out of respect, curiosity, and consent, it is not my place to share my daughter and granddaughter's lived experience; that is their story to tell.

For myself, my story includes relationships with my family of origin and chosen family, with friends—both casual and close—and with colleagues who affirm or do not affirm me, as well as with lovers—past and present-physically, emotionally, and energetically.

Throughout this book, I will share healing insights, erotic lessons, and the healing system I have developed, curated, and used personally and professionally as a crisis and trauma therapist and clinical somatic sexologist who has cared for my clients, my children, and my wounded embodiment and anchored us with an empowering embodiment. This healing system is what I used to SHIFT myself and others from crisis to thriving after surviving active suicidal ideation that was inflamed by a wounded embodiment informed by childhood wounds, the rejections of desirability politics, losses and lessons of life,- all while trying to deal with the pressures of BE-ing and overextending that BE-ing. This healing system is what I have not only taught my clients, but I have personally practiced, integrated as a lifestyle, in addition to teaching to my daughter and to see her teach to my granddaughter.

> "Love is the will to extend oneself for the purpose of nurturing one's own or another's spiritual growth."
>
> *--M. Scott Peck*

I first saw Peck's definition of love in bell hook's book, All About Love. In this book, hooks explains that will implies choice. Therefore, I concluded that one has choice in giving and receiving love. Love is not just an emotion. It is an actionable experience. According to hooks, love comprises of seven attributes: (1) care, (2) affection, (3) recognition, (4) respect, (5) commitment, (6) trust, and (7) honest and open communication. For me, the definition and its attributes gave me clarity, in addition to, tangible measurables when I am discussing, sharing, teaching, and embodying love. I have always said my talent and gift is love. However, I had to develop a new relationship to love starting with self-love and challenging the defaults that informed that love.

The Defaults: The Master's Tools Will Never Dismantle The Master's House

Audre Lorde's powerful words and work, *"The Master's Tools Will Never Dismantle The Master's House"* encourages us to remember centering societal and sexual assumptions and expectations and the systems, what I call "The Defaults", in which they exist will not liberate us. These defaults shames persons and bodies not considered desirable nor respectable. Our individual and collective unlearning of The Defaults are not going to become unlearned by making ourselves despair over those messages. To liberate myself with SHIFT as my personal and professional healing practice, I learned to intentionally challenge, deconstruct, decenter, unpack, and unlearn societal and sexual assumptions and expectations. In my healing, I had to acknowledge that as a descendent of an enslaved Africans on Turtle Island- me and my ancestors you're not seen with our humanity nor with compassion. My liberation was the process of reclaiming my respect, my desires, and with compassion for myself and my ancestry. One of the first things I will encourage you do to is identify "The Defaults" you need to challenge to transform your relationship to love and liberation.

Here is a list of The Defaults and some sample harmful messages that inform societal and sexual expectations and assumptions that you internalize with self-limiting or self-empowering beliefs:

1. **Heteronormativity**

Definition: Heteronormativity refers to the assumption that everyone is heterosexual and this is expected sexual orientation of everyone you meet thus marginalizing and devaluing other sexual attraction orientations.

Self-limiting belief: I must conform to heterosexual norms and expectations to be accepted, respected, and valued.

Empowering belief: My worth and identity are not determined by who I am attracted to, my sexual orientation. I embrace and celebrate the diversity of sexual orientations, including my own.

2. Ableism

Definition: Ableism refers to discrimination, prejudice, and social exclusion against individuals with disabilities, based on the belief that able-bodiedness as "normal" and superior.

Self-limiting belief: I am limited and defined by my disability, and my contributions and value are diminished because of it.

Empowering belief: My worth and potential are not determined by my disability. I have a right to live in an inclusive society that values and respects people of all abilities.

3. Normalcy

Definition: Normalcy is the perception that certain characteristics, behaviors, and identities are the socially accepted standard often excluding those who deviate from this assumption.

Self-limiting belief: I must conform to the socially accepted standard of societal and sexual assumptions and expectations to be accepted and valued.

Empowering belief: I reject the notion of a single definition of normalcy. I honor my uniqueness and celebrate the diversity of identities and experiences in the world.

4. Monogamy

Definition: Monogamy refers to the practice of having a single romantic or sexual partner at a time.

Self-limiting belief: I must adhere to monogamy as the only valid and acceptable relationship model, and this determines my worth, respectability, and desirability.

Empowering belief: I recognize that there are diverse relationship and love styles, and that consensual, ethical non-monogamous relationships are valid and fulfilling. I will choose a relationship model that aligns with my values, needs, and desires.

5. Cisgender

Definition: Cisgender is an adjective used to describe individuals whose gender identity aligns with the sex assigned to them at birth.

Self-limiting belief: My gender identity including my gender performance and gender expression must align with societal expectations and norms to be valid and respected.

Empowering belief: I honor and affirm my authentic gender identity. I can recognize and respect the validity of all gender identities, including transgender and non-binary experiences.

6. Assumed Christianity

Definition: Christianity is a religion centered around the life and teachings of Jesus Christ. For example, within the United States, there is an assumption people are Christians.

Self-limiting belief: My worth and morality are determined solely by adherence to the specific beliefs and practices of Christianity.

Empowering belief: My belief or non-belief of a higher power and corresponding relationship does not have to adhere to any religion. I can embrace the principles of love, compassion, and justice found while recognizing the diversity of spiritual and religious beliefs. I honor my own spiritual journey and respect the beliefs of others.

7. Parental Supremacy

Definition: Parental supremacy is the belief that parents have absolute authority and control over their children, disregarding the child's autonomy and agency, ability to make decisions and ability to act on decisions they can make even with adult supervision and guidance.

Self-limiting belief: I must conform to my parents' expectations and desires to be worthy of their love and acceptance.

Empowering belief: I value and can assert my own autonomy and agency. I recognize that love and acceptance from affirming and compassionate parents should be unconditional and supportive of my growth and self-discovery.

8. Adult Supremacy

Definition: Adult supremacy is the belief that adults are inherently superior to children, teens, and young people, often leading to the dismissal of a youth's perspectives and experiences.

Self-limiting belief: I am less valuable, and my opinions are less valid because of my age and youth.

Empowering belief: I recognize the importance of my voice and perspectives as a young person. I am worthy of respect from my elders and other adults.

9. White Supremacy & The Racial Caste System (U.S.)

Definition: White supremacy refers to the systemic structures, institutions, ideologies, and policies based on racial categories informed by colonization and capitalism that prioritize and empower those perceived as white individuals while marginalizing, penalizing, and restricting individuals who are not white. This racial caste system is informed by anti-Blackness as being of African descent or dark-skinned is perceived as undesirable.

Self-limiting belief: My worth and opportunities are determined by the color of my skin, racialized embodiment, and my racial position within the racial hierarchy.

Empowering belief: I hold no shame of my ancestry and recognize the ancestral and generational value of my heritage and cultural practices.

I will mindfully disrupt, challenge and dismantle white supremacist systems and ideologies that informs my self-limiting beliefs and insecurities. I recognize and celebrate the richness and value of diverse racial and ethnic identities and work towards racial equity and justice.

10. Desirability Politics (i.e., Texturism, Colorism, Sizism, Affluence, Education, etc.)

Definition: To be desired is to be wanted with longing. Desirability politics refers to the social hierarchies and biases based on certain characteristics, such as hair texture, skin color, body size, youth, and educational attainment. These desired attributes are usually informed by White supremacy, its racial caste system, and economics hierarchies of capitalism.

Self-limiting belief: My worth is determined by society's standards of desirability, and I must conform to these standards to be valued.

Empowering belief: I reject the notion that my worth is contingent on conforming to narrow standards of desirability. I embrace and celebrate the diversity of appearances and experiences, valuing myself and others beyond superficial judgments. I am desirable.

11. Respectability Politics (How one behaves, dresses, speaks, acts with or without modesty)

Definition: To be respectable means to behave, dress, speak, and act in accordance to socially desirable norms. Respectability politics refers to the belief that marginalized individuals must conform to dominant societal standards of behavior, appearance, and speech to gain acceptance and respect. These desired attributes are usually informed by White supremacy, patriarchy, and economics hierarchies of capitalism.

Self-limiting belief: I must conform to societal expectations of respectability to be valued and taken seriously.

Empowering belief: I reject the idea that my worth is tied to superficial notions of respectability. I honor and express my authentic self, embracing diverse forms of self-expression and challenging respectability norms.

12. Patriarchy

Definition: Patriarchy refers to a social system where power, preference, and authority are informed and held by heterosexual men, reinforcing gender inequalities and subjugating women, transgender people, and non-heterosexual people.

Self-limiting belief: My value and voice are diminished because of my gender in a patriarchal society.

Empowering belief: I challenge patriarchal systems and ideologies by being my most authentic self. I recognize and affirm the equal worth and rights of all genders, promoting gender equity, and dismantling oppressive gender norms.

13. Assumed Active Sexuality and the Ignoring of Asexuality

Definition: Assumed active sexuality refers to the assumption that everyone experiences sexual debut (i.e. virginity), sexual attraction, and desires sexual relationships, often marginalizing individuals who identify asexual.

Self-limiting belief: My worth and identity are invalidated because of my lack of sexual attraction or desire.

Empowering belief: I embrace and validate my asexuality as a legitimate and valid sexual orientation. I advocate for asexual visibility and recognition, fostering understanding and acceptance of diverse sexual orientations and other types of attraction.

14. Assumed Sexual Debut

Definition: Assumed active sexuality refers to the assumption that everyone experiences sexual attraction and desires sexual relationships, often marginalizing individuals who identify asexual.

Self-limiting belief: My worth and identity are invalidated because of my lack of sexual attraction or desire.

Empowering belief: I embrace and validate my asexuality as a legitimate and valid sexual orientation. I advocate for asexual visibility and recognition, fostering understanding and acceptance of diverse sexual orientations.

15. Assumed Active Sexuality and the Ignoring of Asexuality

Definition: Assumed active sexuality refers to the assumption that everyone experiences sexual attraction and desires sexual relationships, often marginalizing individuals who identify asexual.

Self-limiting belief: My worth and identity are invalidated because of my lack of sexual attraction or desire.

Empowering belief: I embrace and validate my asexuality as a legitimate and valid sexual orientation. I advocate for asexual visibility and recognition, fostering understanding and acceptance of diverse sexual orientations.

"If I didn't define myself for myself, I would be crunched up into other people's fantasies for me and eaten alive."

-Audre Lorde

Impacts of The Defaults

M

y first job graduating from undergraduate school as a social worker was being an individual and family therapist. That was a little over 21 years ago. Some of the common healing themes I saw in the youth and families I supported I saw were safety, parent-child power struggles, compassion-fatigue, relationships, intimate partner violence, gender roles, same gender attraction, desirability, and sexuality. As a novice therapist, I felt unprepared to support my clients regarding some of the specificity of these themes, however, I knew what I could not understand, I could at least have compassion and capacity to support. In deciding to fill my knowledge gaps for myself and curate safe spaces for my clients and myself to explore these themes I continued to pursue a master's degree in social work and eventually, in human sexuality.

In pursuing "higher" education, I recognized how The Defaults that made therapy un-affirming and harmful to folks who did not align with The Defaults, particularly those with marginalized identities.

The impact of these defaults harms those who do not benefit and experience privilege from those defaults. These defaults to our relationships and our ability to show up or be present in our relationships. I witnessed the impact of sexuality and gender conversations causing shame, confusion, and anger. I also witness how the lack of comprehensive sex education in my profession of social work and in practice of social work was still considered taboo. What was also taboo was how to interventions of healing strategies and care practices outside of an Western, Euro-centric, and medicalized were minimized, and not considered as valuable nor impactful. I felt helpless as conventional approaches like cognitive behavior therapy was not addressing how shame, safety, and the inability to self-regulate informed and prevented healing approaches, conversations, and education from happening and most importantly, kept people from healing.

Why is this important? From a sexological worldview or an understanding of the world from a sexuality lens, sexuality is our entire sense of being. It is our emotions, thoughts, beliefs, and behaviors related to one's gender, who we are attracted to, our relationship to pleasure, pain, power and how we live in our body. From a healing-justice perspective, honoring the integrative relationship between our mind and body or embodiment allows us to access safety and self-trust. Without safety and self-trust, we cannot access our peace, our power, nor our pleasure.

This book is informed with the intention of supporting you in challenging those defaults and how they have impacted your ability to create safety from within or embodied safety, develop and sustain self-trust and thrive from your access of your peace, your power, and your pleasure.

This book will provide insights into what to consider when you are challenging those defaults and creating a liberating relationship with yourself while offering a healing-centered framework and system of self-care for the purpose of establishing and embodying safety within yourself and empower your embodiment to disrupt and dissolve shame, self-doubt, and heal wounded embodiment.

Your WHOLE-Self: The Essence and Expression of The Self

The mind is the brain's awareness of The Self, the consciousness. In neuroscience and psychology, consciousness is the awareness of internal and external sensory information of one's self-perception within their relationship of space and time. The awareness of The Self is one's conscious, subconscious, and unconscious perceptions or inner understandings of their mind, body, and spirit. From a sexological worldview, your sexuality is The Self. Do I mean you as just a sexual or asexual being, no. As defined earlier, your sexuality is your entire sense of being. Your sexuality is your emotions, thoughts, beliefs/mindset, and behaviors as related to your gender, who you are attracted to, your relationship to pleasure, pain, power and how you live in your body. Simply, The Self is your WHOLE-Self.

You can further understand your WHOLE-Self by understanding the essence and expression of The Self. The essence or energy of The Self is the energetic totality of your mind, body, and spirit or your aura. The expression of The Self and your aura exists your self-confidence, self-esteem, and self-worth. Your self-confidence is the belief in yourself. Your self-esteem is knowing yourself. From a wholistic point of view, your self-worth is your value as a human being *outside* of The Defaults of societal and sexual assumptions and expectations.

Together- these understandings of your WHOLE-Self become your perception, your embodiment, and your spirit. Your self-confidence, self-esteem, and self-worth are your embodied resources. For post-traumatic growth and healing, these embodied resources, the essence and expression of The Self, requires having radically honest conversations with yourself about your mind, body, and spirit, your WHOLE-Self. SHIFT will teach you how to safely have those healing conversations and to trust the conversations you are having with your WHOLE-Self.

What is embodiment?

Embodiment is the integration of one's mind, body, and spirit informed by one's energetic totality, aura, also known as the energy body. The embodiment of your emotions, your thoughts, your beliefs creates your mindset, and informs your behaviors. As a clinical somatic sexologist supporting trauma survivors, I have come to understand that one's embodiment is also related to one's gender, who one is romantically and sexually attracted to, in addition to, their relationship to their pleasure, their pain, their power and how one lives in their body. This conscious, subconscious, and unconscious perceptions or inner understandings of one's mind, body, energy, and spirit is one's WHOLENESS.

What is a wounded embodiment?

A wounded embodiment is the disassociation and detachment from one's WHOLENESS as one struggles with the inability make decisions in their best interest. One with a wounded embodiment will protect themselves with behaviors like self-sabotage, procrastination, negative self-talk, and second-guessing one's self or self to avoid the hurt and harm of rejection, criticism, and failure. In spite of their highest and greatest goo, a person with a wounded embodiment cannot have a worldview or make decisions from a grounded, present, and intention. A person with a wounded embodiment often experiences self-doubt, anxiety, fear, depression, and feelings of unworthiness and poor self-image. This impacts their self-esteem, self-confidence, and self-worth which is usually informed by their relationship with embodied safety, security, and stability.

What is an empowered embodiment?

An empowered embodiment is a synergy and connection to WHOLENESS as one can make decisions in their best interest for their highest and greatest good and act on the decision. They often experience self-confidence, self-assurance and intuitive in the relationship with their mind, body, and spirit. Safety, security, and stability are foundations with their relationship with their mind, body, and spirit informed by their energetic totality, otherwise known as, aura and energy body (i.e. embodiment).

An empowered embodiment allows one to make decisions from a grounded, present, and intention integrative space of their mind, body, and spirit informed by their energetic totality, otherwise known as, aura and energy body.

What is a marginalized identity?

A marginalized identity is a social, mental, physical, and/or economic characteristic society creates and assigns value to determine one's worth in being respectable and desirable. This perceived sense of value or worth determines the ease or dis-ease of one's lived and erotically lived experience. In a capitalistic society, worth is determined by labor and/or contribution of labor. Worth is determined by capitalistic systems of access and power, in addition to, the persons and societies that benefit from said system. Worth is what one internalizes as self-worth. This self-worth impacts one's self-esteem and self-confidence thus informing one about their embodiment.

What is healing?

Healing is the return to balance and feeling of wholeness of one's emotional, mental, spiritual, sexual, physical, and metaphysical selves. Healing does not mean the absence of pain. Healing is an integrative understanding of oneself from a discerning embodiment of wholeness in relationship to the connection to Self and to others.

This integrative understanding of The Self requires the presence and awareness of the relationship to one's emotional, mental, physical, spiritual, sexual, and metaphysical selves. This integration, coming together or alignment with oneself, is the summation of the relationship of and between our mind, body, and spirit. Healing is homeostasis or balance and integration. Healing allows us to nurture our anger, grief, and sense of helplessness. This allows us to access safety, peace, joy, pleasure, and liberation.

Decolonizing Healing

Decolonizing healing is an intentional and discerning reclamation of wholeness and ancestral knowing supported by kinship and community for the purpose of challenging, deconstructing, decentering, unpacking, and unlearning societal and sexual assumptions and expectations (i.e., The Defaults) rooted in white supremacy, whiteness, and their offspring, capitalism and colonialism. In my personal and professional healing, I committed to this intentional and discerning reclamation of wholeness, ancestral knowing, kinship, and community. I have learned how to center my contemporary, generational, and ancestral lived and erotically lived experiences. In my healing, I realized the importance for myself and my clients to reclaim our power outside of the systems informed by capitalism and colonialism and create healing spaces, internally and environmentally, that were safer. Decolonizing healing can provide a transformative lens to your everyday living.

For this type of healing to take place in the professional spaces I curate for queer and non-queer Black women, femmes, and non-binary folks, I realized to be safer I had to learn how to challenge anti-Blackness, homophobia, transphobia, and the historical treatment and care of sexual violence upon my ancestors ignored. In my professional and teaching work, I found clients and students were also responding to internalized beliefs, mindsets, and ways of being or embodiments reinforced by The Defaults. The healing spaces created challenges much respectability and desirability politics in which we engaged society and ourselves.

Therefore, I encourage you to consider how you will use SHIFT to challenge, deconstruct, decenter, unpack, and unlearn societal and sexual assumptions and expectations, in addition to, the internalized values, messages, beliefs, mindsets, and ways of being which informs your understanding of your WHOLE-Self. One only needs to look at research in neuroplasticity, somatics, and epigenetics or the study of environmental factors impact our mind-body development at an energetic level to see how important it is to have an approach to healing that challenges The Defaults that is individual-driven, community-supportive, generational-inclusive, and wholistic (mind-body-spirit) approach to healing. Otherwise, you may not move from crisis and surviving into thriving and stay in a cyclic pattern of shame and self-doubt. It is with this vision SHIFT, A Self-Liberation Practice was created.

So Beautiful Human…

Welcome to this part of your healing journey!

CHAPTER 1

Healing Is Liberated Living

"The relationship you want requires you to be
PRESENT."

-Mx. Lena Queen, LCSW. M.Ed.

Self-regulation allows for co-regulation.

S

elf-regulation is the ability to manage your emotions, their intensities, and their activations to provide a sense of emotional, mental, spiritual, and physical safety with an intentional connection to Self. Co-regulation is when two or more people can self-regulate, thus interacting safely with each other. *Safely* is the key word I want to emphasize. As a psychiatric social worker and clinical somatic sexologist, I know our ability to regulate largely depends on our ability to be present. This knowing is supported by healing-justice, neuroscience, and relationship and sexological research. To be present means you have a conscious awareness of your mind, body, and energy. This conscious awareness is an intentional knowing and discernment of one's thoughts, emotions, motivations, and behaviors. This discernment allows one to develop a relationship with others based on the relationship with one's intentional awareness of their Self.

Healing conversations are important. The ones you have with yourself, in addition to, the ones you will have with your children, partner(s), and loved ones. For example, using my kinship with my daughter, it is my ability to self-regulate and to observe without judgment or witness my daughter when she is sharing the harm of my mistakes as a parent caused her that allow healing to transform our relationship into kinship. My mistakes were her wounds. As a late teen mom (19), I made mistakes. Those mistakes impacted my daughter, who is now 30, and she has been healing from those mistakes. Part of our healing has been having those healing conversations about those mistakes and me not excusing those mistakes.

I have had to work to become mature to be a witness to HER lived experience. To manage and sit with Uncomfortability, shame and guilt was not easy, but I did it and I did it with self-compassion nor excuses. This is self-regulation. In one recent healing conversation in March 2023, I cried hard and happy tears. To hold space for her, to stay present and accountable, and to love and be loved. It is one of the most humbling and empowering moments you can have with a loved one, in this instance with my adult child. Over the last four years. I have witnessed her make hard choices about her life that has created so much self-love and peace. I know our healing conversations our ability to self-regulate for co-regulation has made liberating impact on her and for us. Our relationship is the impact of self-regulation and co-regulation.

Why liberation? Why use such a term in a book about healing?

Simply because my values are shared values within a community that believes in one's ability to make decisions and one's ability to act on the decisions one makes with enthusiastic consent from a place of being informed with accurate, comprehensive, and minimally unbiased information without causing intentional harm to others or policing of those decisions. That is liberation. Liberation is not given, it is achieved. Liberation is what contemporary sexuality and sociological research shows when it comes to people who live wholeheartedly and with little to no fear from a place of self-compassion and self-permission. When one internalizes that value then one has a liberated embodiment. To internalize is to believe and to act. When you live with that power of your center, you are a self-liberator.

As Tricia Hersey, Founder of The Nap Ministry states, "The body is the site of liberation", I assert that ***healing is how we achieve liberation.*** Creating a healing relationship with yourself allows for space for healing in your relationships to others. Healing helps create and support your internal resources of your conscious awareness and emotional regulation from the nurturing of mind-body-spirit relationship needed for emotional and erotic intelligence. This healing allows for intimacy, vulnerability, and trust to be explored, discovered, eventually embodied thus creating capacity for relationships desired with Self and others.

"I will tell you what freedom means to me! No fear! I mean really no fear…That's the only way I can describe it…that's not all of it… but it is something to really, really feel."

-Nina Simone

CHAPTER 2

Healing 101: Becoming Healing-Centered

I remember the first time I wanted to introduce clients to integrative healing practices like meditation, mindful movement, breathwork and energy work. My clients were primarily teens and adults trauma survivors managing intense emotions and, most times, suicidal ideation that led them to receive inpatient care. I thought my clients *and* my colleagues would think I was uninformed or unprofessional. Practicing in a rural area, healing Practices like these were viewed as fringe in social work and therapy. Conventional social work and therapy was and still is very cognitive behavioral therapy (CBT). According to the American Psychological Association, "CBT therapists emphasize what is going on in the person's current life rather than what led up to their struggles"…and while, only some details about a person's lived experience and their identity was taken into account, "the focus is primarily on moving forward in time to develop more effective ways of coping with life" (Source:http://www.apa.org/ptd-guideline/patients-and-families/cognitive-behavioral.aspx). An integrative approach to trauma work was not mainstream. There were no popular approaches to honor the relationship to mind, body, and spirit that was not centered in Christianity and, at that time, I was not aware of the research regarding post-traumatic growth and healing. However, my education about these integrative healing practices from works by Queen Afua and Dr. Muata Ashby, research about meditation, mindfulness, and transpersonal approaches, and my own personal practice, I knew these healing practices were impactful. That was in 2010.

Despite that professional self-doubt, informed by the knowledge I had, and with my clients' consent, I moved forward. From that, what I saw from my clients were improvements in their ability to connect with hope, feel a sense of their own power, and most importantly, believe in and practice the skill of being in relationship with their intense emotions and their suicidal ideations *safely*. This was phenomenal.

Today, one only needs to look at contemporary studies of epigenetics, the science of how trauma impacts the body individually and generationally, and neuroplasticity, the science of how the mind and body repairs and heals to understand that most times- there is more needed than therapy alone. This is not to say therapy cannot be healing alone. It is to say when more than therapy is needed, you should not be shamed for using your agency and autonomy to make informed decisions to honor, acknowledge, center, and engage in healing practices which area often indigenous to Turtle Island, Africa, South Asia, East Asia, and Pacific Islands. These healing practices are known in Western medicine, as complementary and alternative medicine.

In a 2002 report, White House Commission on Complementary and Alternative Medicine Policy was the first policy to set out to highlight, clarify, and provide guidance to the public and to healthcare professionals regarding practices such as "chiropractic, acupuncture, massage, herbs, and nutritional and mind-body therapies and a host of other approaches" and "prevent chronic illness by teaching…the fundamentals of self-care."

Within the US-healthcare system and particularly for those with marginalized identities within movement spaces, there must be a way to honor the ancestral and historical healing connections to address mental, emotional, spiritual, and physical burnout, complex trauma, and compassion-fatigue.

Becoming Healing-Centered

I use the analogy of healing, like the feeling one has when they are healing from a paper cut. It is itchy, uncomfortable, and sometimes painful; however, instead of scratching and reopening the wound, you manage the discomfort by soothing both yourself and that wound. This is what I witness my clients achieve when they focus on the relationship with their mind, body, and spirit and not just on their therapy and coaching outcomes. With this focused, I confirmed what I intuitively knew- our relationship to our mind, body, and spirit is informed by our lived experience and our ability to access safety and self-trust. One's lived experience was just as important as their ability to feel safe within themselves. This is how I began to become healing-centered. What I knew personally could happen. Your wounds make you feel chaotic; however, being able to manage the discomfort of a healing wound by establishing and embodying the safety and developing self-trust is the process I call "self-liberation".

Healing-justice is a term coined and defined by Southern (U.S.) Black and Native femmes, healers, and reproductive justice movement leaders, co-founder Cara Page and Kindred Southern Healing Justice Collective. Healing-justice means to "honor the historical communal connections within movement and the need for movement spaces to address the mental, emotional, spiritual, and physical burnout and complex trauma" experienced by people, bodies, and communities with marginalized identities. My approach to establishing and embodying safety and creating self-trust is healing-centered. In my healing, personally and professionally, I center the reclamation of sexual, spiritual, energetic, cultural, and other indigenous healing practices with a lens of radical honesty and authenticity. With SHIFT, I encourage you to consider this approach as part of your journey of self-liberation.

For your consideration, I have identified the following healing values. Review the healing values and complete your own value assessment of becoming healing-centered. Scale them from 0-10 of how important of a value it is to you.

0 =Not important at all & 10= Very Important

Here are 18 values of being healing-centered to consider:

1. Healing is both individual and collective.
2. Sensuality, the relationship and nurturing of our senses and our intuition, is self-care.
3. The erotic, or the energy of desirability, both sexual and non-sexual, is the embodiment of our lived experience.
4. There is the importance of joy in healing.
5. Embodying pleasure is important and possible.
6. The reciprocity of emotional labor is important and possible,
7. The power of vulnerability,
8. Being uninhibited/without shame in our pursuit of our needs & our desires is paramount to our ability to thrive.

9. Healing does not look the same for melanated people as it does for non-melanated people.

10. Healing is rest and work.

11. Healing is not about peace but the ability to return to peace.

12. Healing is the heavy lifting of OUR OWN emotional labor.

13. Healing is continuous and layered.

14. It is an ongoing process not rooted in the Western Euro-centric understanding of the body and medicalized symptoms.

15. Healing is about the relationship to mind, body, and spirit.

16. Healing is an integration of one's emotional, spiritual, sexual, mental, physical, and metaphysical selves.

17. Healing is both/and, not either/or.

18. Healing is complicated and compassionate.

A Moment of Self-Reflection:

What would you add? What are some of your healing values?

____

____

____

CHAPTER 3

The Healing Power of Self-Compassion

The Radical Use of Self-Compassion - Nurturing the Seed of Self-Liberation

There is exhaustion that is experienced in mind, body, and spirit. Post-COVID-19 lockdown, we are individually and collectively experiencing chronic exhaustion. You cannot motivate or inspire this exhaustion away. You must learn to take care of yourself because you are exhausted and not okay. In the depths of that exhaustion lies there is the transformative power of self-compassion. Self-compassion is the care and concern you usually extend to others- you extend to yourself- your WHOLE-Self. The radical use of self-compassion is self-kindness and, as a pathway to healing, it paves the way for emotional, mental, physical, spiritual, and metaphysical safety. By extending self-care, self-kindness, self-understanding, and self-love towards yourself, you create a nurturing environment for safety, resilience, growth, and profound healing. SHIFT is not just an embodied healing practice and system of self-care. SHIFT is an embodied movement towards the sacred experience of self-permission, self-compassion, and self-trust to unlock the transformative healing potential that must not become just believable but also embodied.

I first developed SHIFT as a crisis therapist in a child psychiatric center and continued to refine the healing practice in other environments, such as an alternative school for high school students, as well as inpatient and outpatient settings. As a crisis therapist, I often saw how my clients couldn't access the tools offered by traditional therapy because those settings didn't allow them to see themselves compassionately and were supported by professionals experiencing compassion fatigue. Therefore, emotions like shame, guilt, anger, resentment, and disbelief often prevented them from engaging in their care and, ultimately, their healing. I worked to educate clients on establishing and embodying safety with SHIFT. I observed how clients responded and how families found hope. SHIFT was also something they could replicate at home. Eventually, I began teaching colleagues and interns SHIFT, and I saw how this self-care system serves as a healing framework for professionals dealing with compassion fatigue. One of the most important lessons I learned as a psychiatric social worker is that without safety, one cannot connect with oneself to shift intense emotions or the thoughts that accompany those emotions. Additionally, I witnessed that without capacity—personally and professionally—it was difficult to support others' healing. To this day, I carry that wisdom into my private practice, therapy, coaching, and consulting work.

The Healing Power of Self-Compassion

Self-compassion is the care and concern you have shown others, you show yourself. It is self-kindness *and* self-permission. The profound impact of activating self-compassion allows you to engage in deep sense of tenderness, or vulnerability, to witness the intensity of your emotions, safely challenge any shame, guilt, anxiety, and/or other intense emotions by taking care of yourself. When you learn how to hold yourself with such tenderness and give yourself permission to provide *and* receive the care and comfort, you need create a space within yourself that allows for safety and, eventually, where self-trust and healing can be developed, nurtured, and flourished.

Embracing Radical Self-Acceptance with Radical Authenticity and Radical Honesty

What is it to be radical? To be radical is to be unapologetic for being beautifully you.

Trauma disrupts our energy and our ability to connect to that wholeness. As a result of your trauma, you often developed self-depreciating and self-sabotaging ways of being. Being able to acknowledge and confront how those ways of being impacts your ability to be self-compassionate and self-permissive in your healing requires skills that I call radical honesty and radical authenticity. Together, they create an embodiment of radical self-acceptance in which emotions like shame, guilt, anger, and resentment are no longer in control of your ability to take care of yourself.

Radical self-acceptance is the key that unlocks a healing practice of embracing your WHOLE-Self, including your *perceived* flaws, imperfections, and past mistakes. By acknowledging and being in relationship with your vulnerabilities, you free yourself from the oppression of self-judgment and self-criticism. Through radical self-acceptance, you create a safe and non-judgmental space for healing and empowerment, allowing you to release the perception of brokenness and cultivate self-forgiveness and wholeness.

Self-Compassion: Cultivating Self-Kindness

Self-compassion is being kind to yourself. I keep repeating that, don't I? It's that important. Why? Self-kindness is the nourishment that fuels the healing strategies of taking care of yourself with intentional care, compassion, and understanding. By shifting your inner dialogue from self-criticism to self-kindness, you nurture a loving relationship with yourself. You learn to embrace your vulnerabilities, celebrate your strengths, and extend grace to yourself in times of struggle. Through the healing strategy of self-kindness, you establish a foundation of safety, where healing can take root and blossom. Remember the definition of love by psychiatrist M. Scott Peck, Love is "the will to extend one's self for the purpose of nurturing one's own or another's spiritual growth." This is love, self-compassion in action. This is grace.

Building Resilience with Self-Compassion

Resilience is the ability to return to a sense of wholeness from the disruption of life's ebbs and flows. By practicing self-compassion, you develop discernment, self-awareness, and, eventually, wisdom. Resilience is the fruit that grows from the seeds of self-compassion. You will learn to move through your ebbs and flows by using self-compassion as a skill. This will allow you to nurture your ability to take care of you *consistently*. As a healing system, SHIFT contains practical strategies for incorporating self-compassion into your evolving, empowering beliefs, mindset, routines, relationships, and care practices. By integrating self-compassion with your life, you can create a more stable internal resources that will foster a deep sense of safety and connection within yourself.

A Moment of Self-Reflection:

What is your relationship with self-compassion? How often are you gentle with yourself?

CHAPTER 4

From Wounded to Empowered:

Becoming Unstuck

Stuck: To not be able to move

T here are times we get stuck- stuck in our feelings, stuck in our mindsets, stuck in our behaviors. This sense of being stuck can make you feel heavy, lost, and powerless. It feels like "I don't know how", "I don't know what I am doing or "I am just going through the motions". There is this sense of listlessness, no direction. You feel like you are experiencing the same losses REPEATEDLY. Losses as in your lived experiences that have yet to become LESSONS. Moving past stuck requires you examined and, possibly, reframed those "losses" with your conscious awareness of Self and self-compassion. This makes room for learning empowering beliefs, mindsets, and behaviors that become lessons and skills you need to move your healing forward from a wounded sense of self or embodiment to empowered sense of self or embodiment.

A Quick Note: I don't mean losses in the capitalistic sense of win or loss. I mean loss as the embodiment or prospection of loss as in grief and bereavement.

What initially moves a person from losses to lessons, from wounded and out of crisis towards becoming empowered are three embodiment resources. Here are those resources:

First, *desire* your healing. Your relationship to desire to heal signals your relationship to consent and intentionally heal. Establishing and embodying safety and creating self-trust requires an empowered relationship with consent and intention. Consent is how you access self-permission and intention is purpose or reasoning for engaging in your healing. Second, you must *believe* in your ability to heal. Belief is the faith required to create or manifest your healing. Thirdly, you must be willing to activate *self-compassion.* Self-compassion is the kindness and grace needed to dissolve shame and other emotions that leaves you feeling powerless. All require you to have a relationship with VULNERABILITY and the ability to be PRESENT your emotions, mindsets, and behaviors. Your relationship to vulnerability and presence allows you to be connected to yourself and others in ways that can be safe, intimate, trusting, and liberated. I have found the key to these connections are intuition and the relationship to your intuition.

What is your intuition and why is your relationship to your intuition important? Your intuition is your internal guide or GPS informed by your connection to Self and your power. Your intuition is your sense of knowing and discernment, your 6th sense. This knowing and discernment informs your ability to make and trust your decisions (autonomy) and your ability to act on the decisions that you make (agency) without inhibition. When you engage and trust your intuition, you create an embodiment that is no longer informed by self-doubt. With your intuition, you know and trust yourself and eventually learn how to surrender to the unlimited possibilities of your healing and abundance.

Mini- Self-Reflection: *What is your relationship to your intuition, that "something says?"*

To become unstuck means being present and intuitive. To connect to oneself in these ways can be a challenge for those seeking post-traumatic growth and healing. This is because it requires one to be in relationship with the most tender and vulnerable parts of their beliefs, mindsets, and behaviors that is often not liked and often avoided. This is why self-compassion is so important. With self-compassion, being present means you are giving yourself space and grace to listen to your intuition as its challenging intense emotions and self-doubt. Developing this relationship with yourself creates space to develop trust to listen to your intuition. You know-"that something said". Your intuition is your tool of discernment. Self-doubt prevents you from being present with yourself and making the decision(s) needed for your highest and greatest good.

So, how do you take care of yourself and this self-doubt that has become such a large part of your embodiment…Have you ever heard of the healing concept called Shadow Work?

> "Caring for myself is not self-indulgence. It is self-preservation and that is an act of political warfare."
>
> *Audre Lorde*

Shadow Work: The Journey to Trusting One's WHOLE-Self

There is a concept in psychology developed by psychiatrist and founder of psychoanalysis Carl Jung used to describe parts of oneself, one's personality, that usually struggles in ways that can look like self-doubt, self-sabotage, self-depreciating, trauma/protective responses, and insecurities. This concept is called the Shadow. While this part of your personality may be part of your unhealed Self that you may not like or be in denial about, your Shadow is not always something negative or bad. Self-perception is everything. While the Shadow or shadows is known in popular culture for being dark, unwanted, and even evil, I want to disrupt that sentiment. I want to remind you that in the shadow is also where you can rest, grow, find comfort, and protection. To develop a relationship with your Shadow, you must learn how to trust your intuition. SHIFT provides you with a system of care and structure that will allow you to create safety as you explore and develop a healing relationship with your shadow that allows space for self-trust to develop and be sustained.

Unlearning self-doubt, self-limiting beliefs, mindsets, and behaviors informed by The Defaults take time. There are so many moving parts to healing. That is why some become discouraged, overwhelmed, or simply won't try to heal. Within each of us lies inherent consciousness and power waiting to be recognized and harnessed. I encourage you to not give up on yourself nor your healing. This journey of healing your WHOLE-Self by empowering your self-worth, self-confidence, and self-esteem is your path to SHIFT your embodiment from wounded to empowered.

Shadow Work is "the work" of healing.

-*Mx. Lena Queen, LCSW, M.Ed.*

Who Am I?:
Exploring The Relationship between Your Identity and Your Power

Who am I? Most times when I ask clients to answer that question, they frame their answer in relation to others. See example below.

Me as Therapist or Coach: I want you to answer the question. However, there is a catch. I want you to answer the question in relation to YOURSELF.

Client: Okay, gotcha.

Me: Answer the question: Who am I? Remember not to use your roles on others as an answer.

Client: What do you mean? How can I not? I am a mother, wife…oh.

Me: Mmmhmm

Client: (Thinking)…This is actually harder than I thought.

Me: It is not surprising. We have been socialized to see ourselves in relationship to others, not in relationship with ourselves. This is why folks often struggle with connecting to themselves after a breakup or when they lose their job, or when they lose something that gives them social capital or power.

Me: Our work will be for you to answer those questions with ease and from your center without shame or guilt. And if or when you do have those or any other uncomfortable emotions, you will know how to take care of yourself and stay connected to who you are and what is in your best interest.

Client: That would be something I look forward to.

A Moment of Self-Reflection:

Without using your roles to others to answer, please ask yourself & answer the following:

Who AM I?

____

____

____

____

____

____

____

____

____

____

____

CHAPTER 5

Healing Your Core Wounds:

Honoring Vulnerability & Creating a

THRIVING Mindset

Identifying & Transforming Your Core Wounds with Post-Traumatic Growth and Healing

As defined by the Oxford dictionary, thriving is both an adjective, or a word used to describe, and a verb, a word to convey action. Thriving is our ability to continuously grow and flourish, a place from which abundance is created. Not monetary, but in beliefs, thoughts, and actions. Thriving is an energetic state of BE-ing. Neuroscience indicates that humans experience three main states: crisis, survival, and thriving. We can experience these states at any point in our lives. None are fixed. None is out of our reach. Core wounds are the tender spaces within us, shaped by the trauma of our lived experiences and influenced by our learned self-limiting beliefs. It takes courage to confront your pain and explore the depths of your core wounds to reclaim your stolen power and heal the disrupted development. Core wounds are the imprints left by past experiences that influence our perception of ourselves and the world around us. Where you experience resistance of self-doubt, self-sabotage, and self-depreciation, you need to experience healing. By identifying your core wounds, you begin to unravel the pain of helplessness and hopelessness (i.e. despair) and develop a relationship to the thriving embodiment resources of self-permission, self-compassion, intention, and hope. With these embodiment resources, you reclaim your power and create your healing narratives forging a path towards wholeness and liberation.

Embracing Vulnerability: The Gateway to Your Healing

In her TEDx Talk on vulnerability, Brene Brown describes vulnerability as "the ability to be seen, to be heard, to ask for what you need, to talk about how you're feeling and to have hard conversations". Vulnerability is the raw and tender space where our core wounds reside and tells us where the shadow work must take place. In this section, you explore the significance of embracing vulnerability as the first step towards healing. By acknowledging and honoring our vulnerabilities, you create a safe space for emotional growth and begin to unravel the layers that have held us back. Through authenticity and self-compassion, you open yourselves to the transformative power of healing and pave the way for personal evolution.

Recognizing & Challenging Self-Limiting Beliefs

To become connected and strengthen your internal resources of your self-confidence, self-esteem, and self-worth, you must first confront the self-limiting beliefs that prevent you from embodying the healing of those resources. Self-limiting beliefs often stem from the embodiment or internalized believing of negative and oppressive messages, values, assumptions regarding our lived experiences which is a result of societal, sexual, and gendered conditioning, in addition to, negative self-perceptions. When you challenge and disrupt these self-limiting beliefs, understand how they have influenced your thoughts, actions, and sense of self, you can reclaim the embodiment of being WHOLE. Trauma disrupts your connection to wholeness and healing reminds you -you are WHOLE. By challenging the "truths" of our self-limiting beliefs, you take the crucial step toward achieving the post-traumatic growth and healing of and self-liberation.

The Pleasure Principle: Dissolving Scarcity Mindset and Creating an Abundant Mindset

Your mindset is the worldview through which you see yourself and the world around you. Trauma influences a survivor's worldview. Trauma is defined as an extraordinary event or events that overwhelm a person's ability to adapt. When you experience trauma of any kind, you develop a relationship with fear and lack, collectively known as scarcity. Without healing, scarcity shapes how you see yourself and the world. If you do not disrupt your relationship with fear and lack, scarcity becomes your wounded embodiment. To shift from a scarcity mindset to an abundant mindset—where you see endless possibilities for yourself, beyond capitalism, materialism, and wealth—you must be willing to explore your relationship with pleasure, both sexually and non-sexually. You also need to manage the discomfort that comes with challenging your perceptions and mindset about pleasure. With a sustainable healing practice, you can not only identify and challenge limiting beliefs that block your ability to experience pleasure but also learn to reframe your perceptions. This will help you cultivate an empowering and liberating sense of embodiment that opens doors to new opportunities—while maintaining safety and self-trust deepen your connection with others.

Releasing Self-Sabotaging Behaviors

Our behaviors are reflections of our beliefs, our mindsets, and our energy. So many times as a coach and therapist, I am educating clients to see their behaviors as reflections to one's sense of Self, not just as causes for habits, tasks and outcomes. There comes a time when you will need to explore your habits or the patterns of behavior that no longer serve you and the mindsets and energy that inform them. Trauma responses may have protected you in the past and this is important to honor-however, now, you are in a place of your healing where you You must examine the mindsets, habits, and actions that block your ability to trust yourself and connect to your self in ways that are for your highest and greatest good. You will become mindful in your healing journey to identify care practices and healing strategies that align with your most authentic self for your highest and greatest good. By consciously releasing self-sabotaging mindsets and behaviors, you create space for healing transformation and the emergence of your true Self.

Disassociation, Detachment, and Emotional Availability: Embracing the Journey of Post-Traumatic Growth and Healing

Disassociation is a trauma response where a person disconnects from their thoughts, emotions, and even their body. Detachment refers to a lack of emotional connection to oneself, others, or the environment within your embodiment. Confronting our protective behaviors of detachment and disassociation is a transformative effort that helps us heal from trauma's impact. By engaging our embodied resources, we increase our capacity for emotional availability. Emotional availability is a key part of healing, allowing us to safely experience vulnerability, pleasure, and to let go of self-sabotaging behaviors. Post-traumatic growth is just that- the tending, care, advancement, connection, and elevation of your WHOLE Self after experiencing a trauma event. Developing the emotional availability to connect with and manage often unsafe and uncomfortable emotions and mindsets can be both challenging and difficult. Gathering and utilizing your embodied resources is an ongoing journey of post-traumatic growth. Post-traumatic growth requires desire, self-determination, and discipline to stay committed to your path of self-liberation.

Commit to that shit!

-Talena Baker-Herron

Sustainability: Committing to Your Care Practices and Healing Strategies for Release and Liberation

Sustainability is the ability to regularly maintain a practice for a long and consistent period of time. Care practices are the activities, routines, and rituals that supports your emotional, mental, physical, spiritual, sexual, energetic, and environmental well-being. An example of a care practice is taking deep breaths. Healing strategies are the methods in which you complete your care practices. A healing strategy would be knowing your likes and combining it with your care practices. For instance, what time of day would you like to do your care practices or what would help you remember do complete your care practices? Knowing what practice is needed for your healing is only part of this journey. Knowing what care practices work for you and how they work will help you maintain your commitment to your healing practice. Additionally, knowing what it will take for you to remain in your commitment to yourself and your healing is what will help you regularly maintain your care practices and its results for a long and consistent period of time.

One of the things that becomes disheartening in the healing process is the ebb and flow of struggles within our healing. The ebbs of your healing journey can be hurdles to sustaining your care practices. However, it is because of your ebbs that your care practices provide the safety and healing that has you Moving toward self-liberation involves freeing yourself from the chaos of outside factors beyond your control. Experiencing the comfort of focusing on what's within your locus of control demonstrates how your care practices empower you. By using self-compassion, you will engage your care practices with your internal resources—your capacity, capability, and desirability—while developing your self-confidence, self-esteem, and self-worth. This will support your healing efforts. It occurs through cultivating an empowered relationship with Self, along with community care practices and healing strategies that help you release self-limiting beliefs, mindsets, and self-sabotaging behaviors.

The shadow work (i.e. healing work) you do in liberating your WHOLE-Self requires EVERY thing you have learned about yourself to be challenged and deconstructed. According to neuroscience, the mind literally has 60,000-70,000 thoughts a day. By evaluating your core wounds, your core needs, your core desires and learning to move from the center of your best interest with self-compassion, in addition to, committed to your healing with a liberated intention, you will establish a secure and stable foundation for the embodied resources of your self-confidence, self-esteem, and self-worth.

To do this in a way that you experience the transformation you are manifesting, you must be willing to be responsible to your healing. Have you ever wondered what your life would be like if you committed to yourself the way you commit to others?

What would your life look like if you benefited from yourself the way others have?

Understanding Responsibility: Accountability and Ownership in Action

Another healing story and lesson- For parent-child relationships, generational healing is something else when you are being accountable for the harm you have caused. I remember the first time I connected to being present to hear my adult daughter share HER lived experience of being my child and how my mistakes were her trauma. That was almost 3 years ago. You continue to have those conversations. For our relationship, part of our healing has been having those talks about those mistakes and me NOT excusing those mistakes. To listen to her discuss those mistakes and the harm that they caused her is HARD and CLEANSING. I had to work to become MATURE to be a witness to her lived experience and her healing.

Oftentimes you become discouraged in our healing journey. My daughter (32) has been dropping her healing gems on me and the first time I heard it-she was 13 years old. One of those gems is "Commit to that shit." In one of our many healing conversations, she discussed how either someone was an asshole or a saint, one needed to commit, show up in whatever their authenticity is. One of the lessons healing taught is the importance of being genuine and committed to whatever you were doing. For me and in what I teach, it was not enough to compassionately share the importance of being responsible within my commitment to heal. I wanted to create measurable attributes so one would know I am being responsible with that commitment. I measure responsibility with accountability and ownership.

Responsibility is not merely a burden to bear; it is a gift of empowerment. By understanding your relationship to accountability and ownership, responsibility is not an unmeasurable character trait. Responsibility becomes an intention in which your consciously aware of your impact to yourself and to your relationships. I also call responsibility- intentional impact. With intentional impact, you are not focused on the outcome, instead, you are being mindfully present of the moment you are in, the thoughts you are having, the actions you are engaging or avoiding, and the energy you are transcending.

Accountability to Your Healing

Accountability is the awareness and acknowledge of your actions, including past harm caused, and the intention to engage in care practices and healing strategies for the purpose to not repeating harm. Accountability is a measuring tool that guides you on your path of healing, growth, connection, and liberation. Accountability is a commitment to yourself and to those you harmed. With accountability for your actions and their outcomes, you unlock the power to learn from your mistakes, make amends, and evolve into your most authentic self. Accountability becomes the cornerstone upon which you build trust, integrity, and meaningful connections with ourselves and others.

Embracing Ownership: Becoming the Author of Our Lives

Ownership is just that- your connection to your mindset, your behaviors, and your embodiment. Ownership is the key that unlocks our potential for healing our core wounds. In this section, you explore the profound act of embracing ownership over our decisions, experiences, and emotions. By acknowledging that you are the authors of our lives, you reclaim agency and influence over our circumstances. You shed the role of passive spectators and step into the role of empowered creators, shaping our narratives with intention, authenticity, and purpose.

A Moment of Self-Reflection:

What is your relationship with self-sabotage? In what ways do you hold yourself accountable to prevent self-sabotage?

____

____

____

____

____

____

____

____

____

____

____

____

____

____

____

____

____

____

____

SHIFT, A Self-Liberation Practice
Healing the Erotic Self

CHAPTER 6
Embodied Intelligence:
Activating Your Internal Resources of
WHOLENESS

R

esponsibility or accountability and ownership become the building blocks of the life you desire to activate the internal resources of capacity, capability, and desirability, you have to engage and sustain your healing. Capacity refers to your emotional and mental space for witnessing, acknowledging, and identifying your ability to engage in healing and live in your truth. Capability refers to the learning styles and healing strategies you use to send and receive information that informs your healing. Desire is not a simple want. Desire is a longing, something connected to you spiritually/soulfully and energetically. Desire is what you need to thrive. It informs your vitality.

Imagine aligning your choices, your decisions, and your actions with your deeply held values and aspirations informed by what you really want out of life, your life. Creatively, this requires you to access your most vulnerable and tender part- the part that is your desire and to navigate the self-limiting thoughts and beliefs associated with your desires. To access these internal resources, you have engaged in self-reflection rooted in radical honesty and radical authenticity. By consciously steering your life by understanding these internal resources, you begin to center yourself in ways that are no longer imaginative, but real, very very real. Next I will explore the four types of intelligences that inform your wholeness. These principles that have a reciprocal relationship to feeling AND knowing you are desirable- emotional intelligence, erotic intelligence, somatic intelligence- your embodied intelligence.

> "Once you know who you are, you don't'
> have to worry anymore."
>
> *-Nikki Giovanni*

What is Embodied Intelligence?

Embodied means to be embedded in your mind, body, energy, and spirit. Embodied Intelligence is the synergy of emotional intelligence, somatic intelligence, and erotic intelligence. Emotional intelligence is the ability to manage the intensity of your emotions. Skills of emotional intelligence include psychological flexibility, self-regulation, empathy/ emotional safety, building rapport, and maintaining healthy relationships with self and others.

Healing the integration of your embodied intelligence creates an empowered self. This is how you SHIFT from wounded to empowered. The process of healing is called *shadow work*. You may have heard of it. Shadow work is an ancestral way of becoming literate in oneself, parts, and WHOLE. Your shadow includes some of the most vulnerable parts. of you that shows up as self-doubt, self-sabotage, self-deprecating, and overall self-perception.

Mini-Self-Reflection: Do you see yourself as desirable?

Unlearn what you know about desire and see desire from your center. The center of putting what is in your best interest as your priority, and what you want from a soulfulness that is needed for you to thrive.

Desirability,sexual and non-sexual, rooted in consent and the authenticity to be present and engaged, is an essential aspect of your journey towards experiencing fulfillment. By honoring your core needs and desires, you create a life that aligns with your authentic values, aspirations, and innermost dreams. With curiosity and wonder, be willing to explore the realm of desirability and uncover the path to a life of authenticity and fulfillment. By challenging the impact of The Defaults and the layers of societal expectations and assumptions, you will connect and be guided by your desires in a way that will be in alignment with your mind, body, and spirit - your embodiment.

Your Mental and Emotional Well-Being: Capacity, Capability, & Desirability

Within the depths of your being lies an expansive reservoir of capacity, encompassing our mental and emotional space and labor. When you embark on a journey of self-liberation to embrace and expand your capacity, you are in the post-traumatic growth to nurture your mental and emotional well-being. You lay a trusting foundation for post-traumatic growth, resilience, healing, and the ability to handle the discomfort of life's challenges and opportunities with self-assurance.

Understanding Capacity: The Essence of Mental and Emotional Space

Capacity is the container that holds our thoughts, emotions, and experiences. Healing requires you to delve into the intricacies of your mental and emotional space, gaining a deeper understanding of its vastness and tenderness. By exploring the factors that influence your capacity, such as trauma, the chronic stress of capitalism and colonial, self-care, and ability to set boundaries, you learn how to fortify your mental and emotional well-being for a more pleasurable and fulfilling life. Your mental well-being is essential for harnessing your capacity to its fullest potential. By implementing a system of care that integrates care practices like mindfulness practices, meditation, positive self-talk, and managing stress in your activities of daily living, you will discover your ability to create and sustain mental resilience, emotional safety, and overall well-being.

Your Emotionality: Embracing Emotional Intelligence

According to Wikipedia.com, emotional intelligence is "the ability to perceive, understand, use, manage, and handle emotions", both yours and others. The realm of emotional intelligence includes the skills of self-awareness, self-regulation, empathy, and social awareness. Emotional intelligence forms the bedrock of our capacity to navigate the complexities of our emotions and relationships. By developing these emotional skills, you enhance your capacity to understand and manage your emotions, build meaningful connections with your Self and others, and communicate effectively.

Strengthening Your Emotional Space: Building Resilience

Resilience is the cornerstone to SUSTAIN your emotional capacity, enabling you to bounce back from trauma and adversity and thrive in the face of challenges. In my professional work, I often support trauma survivors who are learning for the first time how their embodiment has become a personality that protects their emotionality from harm. Our collaborative healing work delves into the healing strategies and care practices that protect their emotional space and expand their capacity for post-traumatic growth.

Through discovering, learning, and implementing healing emotions like gratitude, and cultivating an abundance mindset, you learn to embrace self-compassion and be receptive to support. This process helps you build and internalize resilience, enabling you to learn from and integrate lessons that would have otherwise been internalized as losses.

Tapping into Your Capability - Unlocking Your Cognitive Potential & Exploring Your Unique Learning Style

According to CollinsDictionary.com, cognitive means it's the brain's relationship to learning, knowing, and understanding information. Your capability is your learning style, learning process, and learning comprehension. In the realm of post-traumatic growth, your capability to receive, process, and learn information and concepts plays a pivotal role. Your journey of exploration and discovery of Self by understanding your learning style. Clients are often surprised when I ask about their learning styles. However, I learned early in my career as a social worker and therapist, a person's learning style impacts their ability to receive, process, and understand the information I am providing. Your learning style is something probably known to you, but not often made room for. To unlock your learning ability, your cognitive ability and potential has to be known to YOU. By understanding your unique way of absorbing knowledge, you tap into your truest healing and WHOLE-Self potential and enhance your ability to navigate life's complexities with wisdom and discernment.

Discernment – the ability to judge well.

-Oxford Languages

Each of us has a distinctive way of receiving and processing information. Explore your learning styles and identify your own preferred way of doing things. Whether your learning is visual, auditory, kinesthetic/action/hands-on, or a combination thereof, explore the related strengths and challenges associated with each of your learning styles. By embracing your unique learning style, you unlock your brain's potential and create a nurturing environment for post-traumatic growth and healing.

Embracing Healing as Lifelong Learning

My clients are often frustrated when they seem to have conquered some amazing internal challenges only to be faced with self-doubt or hurt due to things outside of their control. This is where I want to encourage you as I have encouraged them…and myself. Healing is a lifelong learning. Life will ebb and flow. Ebbs are when life seems to have challenges, disappointments, heartaches and unwelcome surprises.

Flows is when you are managing and conquering those challenges, disappointments, etc. with self-compassion, self-trust, and self-belief. Impacted by both your lived experience, your embodiment including your internal resources, and capitalism, learning is a lifelong journey that is informed by your capability and expands your horizons.

Understanding this allows you to explore and connect with a liberating embodiment informed by healing, pleasure, rest, and fulfillment without shame and/or anxiety further and successfully. Your ability to access and discover the transformative power of lifelong learning and its profound impact on our capability to adapt and thrive in an ever-changing world.

Critical Thinking

Critical thinking is the cornerstone of your cognition or brain's ability to receive and process information enabling you to analyze, evaluate, and make informed and discerning decisions. As you shift your healing and embodiment, the art of critical thinking requires discernment in choosing healing strategies and techniques that enhance your ability to question, reason, and problem-solve. This allows you to discard inaccurate and false information. By honing your critical thinking skills, you empower yourself to navigate complex emotions, oppressive assumptions, and expectations to overcome obstacles and make choices aligned with your highest and greatest good. This is how your ability to be discerning is developed.

What is Somatic Intelligence?

Somatic intelligence refers to *the ability to listen AND respond to your mind, body, and energetic responses to your needs and desire for safety, intimacy, and connection.* It involves recognizing and responding to your thoughts, emotional sensations, and physical sensations, and their energy flows to make decisions that support their overall health. Somatic intelligence refers to the body's innate capacity for self-regulation, healing, and knowing. It acknowledges that trauma, stress, and societal oppression are not just mental experiences but are deeply held in the body, manifesting as mistrust of self and others, chronic tension, pain, dissociation, or dysregulation of the nervous system. Just as emotional intelligence requires somatic intelligence, somatic intelligence requires emotional intelligence. In the context of healing justice, the body is not only a site of trauma but also a site of resistance, transformation, and self-liberation.

 In the context of sexuality, somatic intelligence helps individuals heal and improve their awareness of pleasure, boundaries, and sexual identity by tuning into how their body communicates through sensation and movement. Informed by your emotional intelligence, somatic intelligence is your ability to manage your responses and reactions to your inner world.

Embracing Creativity in Your Healing

The constant demand of your emotional and mental labor removes opportunities for creativity. Ever had a time when you just daydreamed? You were able to access a part of you that imagined a different world, a different you. Creativity can be a catalyst for expanding your cognition and learning potential and unlocking new possibilities. Stay mindful of your creativity, its power, and its role in reframing your perspective, generating new awareness, and understanding, and embracing living liberated. Nurturing a creative mindset and exploring healing strategies and practices new to you, you awaken your capability to think outside the box, choose healing practices that you will enjoy and want to do consistently. This will help sustain the outcomes your healing and liberated living creates.

Erotic Intelligence: Honoring Your Core Needs and Your Core Desires

What is Erotic Intelligence?

According to The Center for Erotic Intelligence, eroticism is "the interplay of desire and arousal with the daily challenges of living and loving". Erotic intelligence is the ability to navigate that interplay and those challenges. The Center also shares the five main elements of erotic intelligence are: (1) body attunement, (2) social intelligence, (3) emotional intelligence, (4) "self-awareness on steroids", which to me is a *presence practice* and (5) creative imagination, or what I call *erotic curiosity*.

Body Attunement is the ability to *listen* AND *respond* to your mind, body, and energetic responses to your needs and desire for safety, intimacy (i.e. validation), and connection (i.e. somatic intelligence).

Emotional Intelligence is the ability managing *your* emotions, thoughts, and beliefs that is informed by one's mindfulness, self-regulation, emotional regulation, and intra and interpersonal relationships.

Social Intelligence is the ability to empathetically hold space for others while navigating power dynamics, thoughts, feelings, and behaviors between self and others (i.e. relationship skills).

Presence Practice is a discerning, intuitive understanding of your self-awareness, decision-making process, intention, and this erotic embodiment influences the quality of your self-image, your pleasure. your relationships & your life.

Creative Imagination is your *erotic curiosity* to explore your relationship to your erotic power (i.e. authentic consent) and ability to safely and confidently express your needs, desires, consent-informed boundaries to discover and experience un-inhibited pleasure.

When I interpret how this ability and its elements show up in one's lovership, **erotic intelligence is the intuitive and discerning ability to navigate love, desire, intimacy, and your erotic power with authenticity and erotic curiosity in your everyday life.** Erotic intelligence requires the literacy of the intuitive mind-body-spirit relationship interacting with one's sexual and non-sexual self-awareness to their senses, pleasure, and desirability (i.e. erotic presence practice). Your lovership is your erotic presence practice.

To create capacity for such a relationship, I have learned to explore both the somatic intelligence and embodied intelligence as integrative components of and to access erotic intelligence. Both will be introduced below with care practice recommendations for each.

I once worked with an educator who shared, "Literacy means incorporating reading, writing, speaking, and critical thinking." Literacy seemed like an appropriate word to explain how we put our integrative intelligence to use, and in this case, not just erotic literacy…self-literacy via the erotic. Erotic intelligence is the ability to discern our desires, both sexual and non-sexual, with skills of self-awareness, self-compassion, self-regulation, empathy, and social and relationship awareness and intimate connection.

What we know about desire has usually been taught to us. We have been told that erotic is sexual only. However, the erotic is not just sexual because desire is not just sexual. The erotic is the energy of desirability, both sexual and non-sexual. And from that teaching we have been taught what is respectable, what is success, what has affluence or social capital, and what has value. We have been taught to reach for someone's dreams and expectations for us- for another's desires, not our own.

One of the questions I ask my clients when they are struggling with achieving their goals is "Whose measuring stick are you using?" It was one of the first questions that will have you thinking about whose values, beliefs, assumptions, and expectations you are considering AND are they YOURS?

It is difficult to make decisions when your values, beliefs, and desires are not acknowledged. Often, we move from a place where we were told there is inadequacy in us, so what we want should be outside of ourselves to be considered valuable—both to ourselves and others. We have been taught that having our own vision of self is selfish, deviant, and impulsive. We have been taught not to trust ourselves and our desires.

Embracing Consent: The Power of Free Will and Choice

Consent is the foundation of desirability. Consent is the ability to make decisions (autonomy) and the ability to act on the decision (agency) in which one makes. This is the giving of permission for something to be done or experienced. If you don't want it, it is not consent. Without consent, there is no safety to empower yourselves to make conscious choices aligned with your authentic desires. By understanding the power of consent, you reclaim autonomy and agency over your lives with boundaries that protect your well-being and honor your true desires and needs.

Embracing Alignment & Progress: Liberation from the Illusion of Perfection

In the liberated living of alignment, you will find liberation from the pressure of perfection. You will grant yourself permission to explore, to make mistakes, and to learn from them. You will honor your healing journey, savoring every step forward, regardless of its perceived imperfection- the ebbs rather than the flows. Progress becomes a testament to your commitment to your healing reminding you that your self-worth is not contingent upon external validation but resides within you.

So, let's celebrate progress over perfection. Embrace the messy, imperfect, and beautifully authenticity of your human existence. With each intentional effort, you curate a path created by self-compassion, self-assurance, and an unwavering belief in your whole self.

A Moment of Self-Reflection Exercise:

"Whose measuring stick are you using?" Identify at least one (1) core value regarding your relationship emotional intelligence, erotic intelligence, somatic intelligence, and embodied intelligence.

CHAPTER 7

Developing a Presence Practice: Becoming a Self-Liberator

L

ike most of us, the last few years have been a lot to navigate. For me, compounded by the impact of a premenopausal body and the global pandemic of COVID-19, I experienced changes that were outside of my control. I had to learn how to be present in my power with awareness and self-compassion. As personal and professional WHOLE-Self healing and Self-Liberators, we are in a position to no longer ignore the impact of The Defaults and reconnect to our ability to access joy and bliss, an embodied sense of pleasure and wonderment. I want to remind you that you are WHOLE. Trauma disrupts our connection to feeling whole. Our bodies literally are self-healers with ways and internal mechanisms for healing. In teaching clients how to SHIFT, it became important to educate them about how healing works. For this, I concentrate on three things-a presence practice, neuroplasticity and energy healing.

Developing a Presence Practice

When creating embodied safety and trust with relationships, either with ourselves or with our loved ones, we need to be in relationship with our ability to be discerning via capacity, capability, and desirability.

1. Capacity is our mental and emotional space to be present.

2. Capability is our ability to receive and process what's communicated.

3. Desirability is not only being wanted, it is what one wants.

In order to create such an embodiment, I am encouraging you to develop a presence practice you can do with ease and effort with system of self-care and healing routines you can practice daily, weekly, monthly, and yearly. What do I mean by presence?

Your Presence Practice is

   A. *Awareness* - Your ability to receive and process information through your 5 senses and your intuition, your 6th sense.

   B. *Intention* -A deliberate purpose of the moment, activity, or event you are currently.

   C. *Effort-* the commitment of intentional action through the movement of your mindset (decision-making process), moods, and movements (behaviors).

Activating your presence practice is how you move your lovership from awareness/activation to mindfulness to erotic mindfulness. With self-compassion and curiosity within your day-to-day interactions, using SHIFT, you will pay attention to how your emotional sensations cause bodily sensations and thoughts, and develop empowered ways of developing and sustaining intimacy within your relationships with Self and your loved ones.

Neuroplasticity: The Science of Healing

Neuroplasticity is the scientific term that describes your body's amazing ability to heal by deactivating and/or changing existing behaviors and thinking via creating new neuron pathways. Neurons are just another way of describing brain cells. When you learn new things like how to dissolve self-limiting beliefs or practice a skill like creating an empowering belief or learn a new language, your brain forms new connections between its cells. These connections build a network that works together to allow different parts of your mind and body to communicate and work together. Neuroplasticity is foundational when it comes to healing. This is the "how" healing works. When you are ready (i.e., self-permission/consent), your neuroplasticity is what allows you to create an empowered embodiment for post-traumatic growth and healing. This means with self-belief, self-compassion, time, and practice, you can heal your wounded embodiment. Using care practices that are within SHIFT have been shown to assist in activating and sustaining the healing of neuroplasticity. This is what informs SHIFT as an integrative healing practice.

When I Get That Feeling: Sexual Healing through Somatic Understanding, Neuroplasticity, and the Polyvagal Theory

Defined by research sexologist Dr. Shemeka Thorpe. Ph.D. sexual distress is "negative emotional responses such as worry, anxiety, frustration, bother, or feelings of inadequacy that people experience related to their sex lives and sexual functioning" (Instagram @DrShemeka, 2023). The healing of sexual distress is not the absence of emotional discomfort or psychosomatic pain. Healing is the ability to return to homeostasis or balance. Balance being the ability to manage the intensity of pain and discomfort caused by sexual distress. Healing sexual distress is sexual healing. Sexual healing is the therapeutic. spiritual. and emotional transformation of one's erotic energy (Meyers. 2014).

Sexual healing acknowledges that trauma, shame, or discomfort in our sexual experiences often lives in our bodies, not just in our minds. Somatic healing is a deeply personal journey involving mind, body, and spirit. Neuroplasticity is the body's nervous system ability to repair itself. Trauma sits in our nervous system. The integration of the 5 Stages of Neuroplastic Healing and the Polyvagal Theory offers a profound way to understand and heal our sexual selves. When combined, these approaches provide a roadmap for reclaiming your body, redefining pleasure, and fostering emotional safety.

The 5 Stages of Neuroplastic Healing (**Neuroplasticity**)

Neuroplasticity refers to the brain's and body's ability to reorganize itself by forming new neural connections. When it comes to sexual healing, applying the principles of neuroplastic healing allows us to gradually rewire trauma, shame, or negative associations around sex and intimacy. The five stages include:

I. Neurorepair: This involves identifying areas in the brain and body affected by past trauma or unhealthy experiences. For sexual healing, this could mean recognizing body parts or sexual expressions that trigger discomfort or dissociation. My erotic intelligent workbook, **Healing the Erotic Self (HTES)**, and Erotic **Living Course,** Healing Your Erotic Energy (HYER): The 7-Day Energy Healing Practice, assist in neurorepair.

II. Sequencing: Healing happens in phases, requiring you to address one layer at a time. You might start by focusing on self-compassion before moving toward more intimate practices. A somatic practice like SHIFT

Somatic Healing Practice will help you develop a self-compassionate presence practice.

III. Neurostimulation: This stage encourages engagement with stimulating activities that promote brain and body connectivity. Erotic Breathwork, erotic touch, safe self-pleasure, or sensual dance can help rebuild a positive connection between your mind and body. SHIFT Meditation, HTES 6-week healing intensive, Healing Your Erotic Energy (HYER) 7-Day Energy Healing Practice, and Erotic Activation Breathwork Practice explore solo and partnered erosomatic practices that support this connection.

IV. Neuromodulation: This phase involves regulating stress responses to sexual experiences. Breathing techniques or grounding exercises can help create calm, enabling you to stay present during intimate moments rather than dissociating. One of HTES foundational practice is the Erotic Intelligence Erotic Breathwork Practice, in addition to, trauma release movements and stretching, and erotic affirmations will help you regulate your trauma and stress responses. Make sure you attend the monthly SHIFT and erotic breathwork session.

V. Neurorelaxation & Neurodifferentiation: In this final stage, you learn to relax and differentiate between past trauma and present experiences, allowing you to explore your sexual desires without being driven by old patterns or fears. This is the integration process and will be explored and experienced through the the Liberated Living course of the HTES coaching.

Understanding the Polyvagal Theory in Sexual Healing

The Polyvagal Theory, developed by Dr. Stephen Porges, explains how the vagus nerve plays a crucial role in regulating emotional responses, especially during intimate or vulnerable moments. The vagus nerve is NOT just one nerve but "a family of neural pathways" that communicate sensory information from the body to the brain and motor/movement/behavior information from the brain to the body (Dana, 2020, p. 12). This science informs why somatic practices are transformational for healing, change and transformation.

The 3 principles of the Polyvagal Theory include:

A. Autonomic hierarchy or self-regulation

B. Neuroception or intuition (for the ability to trust)

C. Co-regulation

Autonomic Hierarchy (Self-Regulation):

This refers to the different states of the autonomic nervous system (ANS), which governs our responses to stress and safety. The hierarchy consists of three states: the ventral vagal state (safety and social engagement), sympathetic state (fight or flight), and dorsal vagal state (shutdown or freeze). Self-regulation is the ability to move between these states and manage stress to maintain balance and well-being.

Neuroception (Intuitive Ability): Neuroception is the brain's subconscious ability to detect safety or danger in the environment, through cues from people, situations, or even bodily sensations. This process happens automatically, helping to regulate our autonomic responses (such as activating fight/flight or calming down). When recognizable about our conscious awareness, this subconscious awareness evolves to become our intuition.

Co-Regulation:

Co-regulation is the process by which individuals regulate each other's emotional and physiological states through connection and being in relationships. It happens when one person's calm and attuned presence helps another feel safe, reducing stress and fostering connection and intimacy.

A Deeper Dive: Autonomic hierarchy for Self-Regulation

Our autonomic nervous system has two branches: parasympathetic and sympathetic nervous systems.

Ventral Vagal State (Safe & Social/Thriving):

This part of the parasympathetic system and is where you feel safe, connected, and open to intimacy. For sexual healing, creating sustainable embodied safety within your body and mind allows pleasure and connection to flourish.

Sympathetic State (Fight, Flight, Fawn/Surviving or Crisis):

When triggered by fear, shame, or past trauma, your body may go into a heightened state of anxiety or hyperarousal. Learning to identify when you're in this state is critical for recognizing when you're feeling unsafe during intimate encounters.

Dorsal Vagal State (Shutdown or Freeze/Crisis or Surviving):

This is the second part of the parasympathetic system. When overwhelmed, your body may dissociate or "shut down" to protect itself. This can manifest as numbness, disinterest in sex, or an inability to experience pleasure.

Understanding why care practices work or don't work through the lens and healing science of neuroplasticity, your sexual healing practice will help you recognize and regulate your body's responses, making space for healing, intimacy, and pleasure. Later in the book I provide example erotic care practices that will support your sexual healing.

Healing your sexual self through somatic practices, the 5 stages of neuroplastic healing, and an understanding of the Polyvagal Theory allows you to reclaim your body, mind, and pleasure. By recognizing the body's responses and nurturing them with compassionate care, you can create a new narrative of embodied safety and self-trust for sexual healing and sexual liberation.

Understanding Energy as Emotions: How the Body Responds to Emotions

Emotional Sensations	**Physical Sensations**
Anxiety	Nauseous, queasy, dizzy
Anger	Hot, explosive, impulsive
Fear/Scared	Cold, trembling, tense
Apprehension/Anticipating	Tingling, jumpy
Shame	Empty, disconnected
Energized	Floating, bubbly
Tender	Moved, touched, warm
Hurt	Sensitive, awful, wobbly
Vulnerable	Open, tender, raw, achy
Constricted	Blocked, clenched, stuck
Jealous	Furious, frustrated
Sad	Abandoned, bored, sleepy
Peaceful	Accepted, calm, connected
Distrustful	Skeptical, suspicious
Confident	Strong, worthy, important
Joyful/Happy	Cheerful, excited, hopeful
Guilty	Conflicted, remorseful

It's your body's nervous system that creates and sends electrical impulses (i.e. energy) throughout your body in response to both internal and external experiences. Your emotions are literally energy in motion stored all through your body.

Did you know there are 27 distinct categories of emotions with thousands of body sensations a person can experience?

Writer Yasmin Anwar for UC Berkeley's Greater Good Magazine wrote an article on this very fact. Those categories are admiration, adoration, aesthetic appreciation, amusement, anger, anxiety, awe, awkwardness, boredom, calmness, confusion, contempt, craving, disappointment, disgust, empathic pain, entrancement, envy, excitement, fear, guilt, horror, interest, joy, nostalgia, pride, relief, romance, sadness, satisfaction, sexual desire, surprise, sympathy, and triumph.

A Moment of Self-Reflection

What are your thoughts on learning about the different categories of emotions and having thousands of body sensations?

____

____

____

____

____

____

____

____

____

____

____

Trauma Responses, A Refresher: Fight, Flight, Freeze, and Fawn

When our nervous system has been harmed beyond its capacity is the impact of trauma. Trauma is defined as an event or disturbance that causes significant distress or impairment in a person's ability to function which impacts their personal, social, and/or relationship interactions. When you experience trauma, your mind and body develop responses that keep you safe. These responses are called trauma responses. Below is a description of 4 types of trauma response.

Types of Trauma Responses:

1. **Fight**
   a. Fight refers to your ability to confront threats in a very straightforward manner.
   b. An example of fight response would be:
      i. Someone offers feedback on your presentation because you have been hurt by being bullied

by others (peers, family, etc.), your body become tense, you internalize the feedback with self-negative thinking "I am always wrong", and you tell them angrily, "I didn't ask for your opinion."

2. **Flight**

    a. Flight refers to your ability to run away or ignore threats.

    b. An example of flight response would be:

        i. A close friend repeatedly texts you that they are stressed out about an upcoming event that you are looking forward to and asks you not to go and hang with them. However, you want to go to the event. Since you don't want to disappoint them by sharing your excitement and intention of attending, you do not share how you are looking forward to the event and avoid saying "no" that you are not able to hang out with them because you would like to attend the event.

3. **Freeze**

    a. Freeze refers to your inability to make decisions and/or feeling stuck.

    b. An example of a freeze response:

        i. You are talking to friends at the dinner table and a loud noise happens and startles you. You are unable to continue in the conversation you were having with your friends and lost track of time and what you were going to say.

4. **Fawn**

    a. Fawn refers to your inability to share your thoughts, so you are overly agreeable or complimentary to others usually out of fear of being mistreated.

    b. An example of a fawn response:

        i. You are at home scrolling on your phone and an adult is in the same room and shares their opinion about social media. You don't want to be look at as disrespectful and worried about being yelled at so you agree with them to avoid being mistreated.

The Energy Centers: Your Embodied Power (Quite Literally)

Did you know that your body has energy centers? In ancestral medicine, these are called chakras (Sanskrit), Ka (Kemetic/Ancient Egypt), and Dantian (Chinese medicine). These energy centers are spinning fields of energy stemming from our body's endocrine system, a network of hormonal glands that not only regulate physical functions but also influence our understanding of The Self through thoughts and behaviors. The energy centers support our physical, emotional, mental, and metaphysical well-being. According to ancestral medicine, there are hundreds of energy centers, with eight major ones. Confirmed by psychiatrist and researcher David Hawkins, M.D., Ph.D., these centers create your energy body or aura, with specific levels of consciousness, often expressed as emotions measured in frequencies. There is too much information to cover all about our energy centers, but I will introduce what they are and how you can use them to map and develop care plans for your healing.

Seven of the eight energy centers are located within your endocrine or hormonal system along your spine with, according to neuroscientist Dr. Joe Dispenza, the eighth energy center is located 16 inches above your head. According to neuroscience, the study of the nervous system, energy centers are part of the body's autonomic nervous system, which is responsible for regulating involuntary functions, such as heartbeat, eye blinking, food digestion, and hormonal levels.

Try this visualization. Imagine your body as a house, and the energy centers are the rooms inside. Each room serves a different purpose with their hormones, own consciousness, and has its own unique frequency and intention. These energy centers communicate to you and inform not only how your mind and body works and feels but also how your consciousness and mindset is developed and beliefs are embodied.

Why is this information important and how does it apply to you becoming self-liberated? Well, too often we are connected to a physicality/body we have no or little working knowledge about. Additionally, The Defaults prevent us from accessing medically accurate, science-based information that tells us HOW healing works. You know not only what societal messages and systems prevent you from accessing your healing, but expanding your knowledge based on how your body works and its relationship to your mind and spirit, empowers you. Period.

This is the both/and of healing. The external world and the internal world create space for integration and eventually synergy...from YOUR CENTER.

Now that you have this information- let me share how you can use this information to shift your healing.

Identifying Your Healing Themes with The Energy Centers

In my professional and personal healing practices, I use energy centers to map how to prioritize healing and shadow work. As mentioned earlier, each energy center's level of consciousness provides healing knowledge specific to each energy center. The healing knowledge includes energy (i.e., vibrational) frequency, level of awareness, healing themes, and healing processes.

Use the list below to identify your healing theme and determine where you are struggling and what healing theme(s) needs your immediate attention:

Your Body's Energy Centers

Energy Center	Healing Theme
1st Energy Center Location: Just below tail bone	Safety, Security, and Stability (Feminine Energy)
2nd Energy Center Location: Pelvic area	Creativity & Desirability, Self-Worth (Masculine Energy)
3rd Energy Center Location: Abdomen	Connection, Self-Confidence, Intuition, "Gut Feeling" (Feminine Energy)
4th Energy Center Location: Heart	Love, Hope, Optimism, Self-Compassion, Magnetism (Masculine Energy)
5th Energy Center Location: Throat	Truth and Communication (Feminine Energy)
6th Energy Center Location: Between brows	Self-Awareness, Self-Esteem, and Discernment (Neutral Energy)
7th Energy Center Location: Top center of head	Self as Source, Self-Assured, Divinity (Neutral Energy)
8th Energy Center Location: 12 ft above you	Connection to the Cosmos, Epiphanies, Downloads (Neutral Energy)

Three Types of Energy Healing Intensions: Cleanse, Protect, Replenish

The three types of energy intentions have specific energetic impacts. An intention is the specified purpose behind an action. An intention not only provides purpose but also clarity and focus. It involves being deliberate, mindful, and consciously aware of the present moment. Through this system of self-care and healing, you activate the body's natural ability to heal, known as neuroplasticity. There are three healing practices that embody the intention behind your care choices and the healing goals you seek: cleanse, protect, and replenish. While these practices are specific to each energy center, SHIFT can also be a form of energy healing for your entire being.

Below is a quick overview of each intention and something to be mindful of as you choose which SHIFT Somatic Healing Practice you engage:

Cleansing your energy centers involves removing any negative or stagnant energy that may be blocking the flow of healing energy. This intention and practice will look like you challenging reframing negative thoughts with Care Practice 4 Affirm of SHIFT or establishing safety with Care Practice 1 Ground of SHIFT.

To protect your energy centers, think of it as putting a shield around your energy. This shield helps keep out anything that could drain your energy or make you feel drained, powerless, and/or unbalanced. Examples of protective practices include a 10-minute gratitude practice, breathwork, or self-reiki. Protective practices are great in helping you take care of yourself. You can do this with Care Practice 3 Nurture of SHIFT.

And just as you replenish your body with food and water, you can also replenish your energy centers. Pour into your empty cup. This will look like you remembering your power with Care Practice 2 Center of SHIFT by asking yourself clarifying questions to do what is in your best interest or mindful movements like stretching for Care Practice 3 Nurture of SHIFT.

There is so much more to know about energy and energy healing. However, for now, remember, your energy centers are your source of safety, power and vitality. With intentions, your care practices and healing strategies will shift your energy to challenge self-limiting beliefs, improve your mood, mindset, and embodiment. By understanding and taking care of your energy, you can unlock your full potential and live a more balanced and energized life.

Energy Consciousness: Your Hormonal Glands

Energy Center	Healing Themes
1st Energy Center Adrenals and Reproductive Glands	Safety, Sexuality, & Elimination
2nd Energy Center Adrenals and Reproductive Glands	Longing, Digestion, Consumption, Processing, and Release
3rd Energy Center Pancreas & Digestive Glands	Stress, Digestion, Consumption, Processing, and Release
4th Energy Center Thymus Gland	Expansion, Repair, and Regeneration
5th Energy Center Thyroid Gland	Metabolism
6th Energy Center Pituitary Gland	Door to Inner Self-Consciousness
7th Energy Center Pineal Gland	Door to Higher Consciousness
8th Energy Center	Access to Quantum Field Memory

Embodied Healing: Becoming a Self-Liberator

As defined earlier in the book, embodiment is the integration of one's mind, body, and spirit informed by one's energetic totality or aura. Healing is the balance and feeling of wholeness of one's emotional, mental, spiritual, sexual, physical, and metaphysical selves. Healing is an integrative understanding of oneself from a discerning embodiment of wholeness and connection to Self and to others.

Embodied healing requires you to be aligned in your mind and body. Within your body, your heart is the magnetic center that draws the energy of unlimited possibilities towards you. Your mind creates the thoughts and relationship to thoughts (I.e., awareness) with your conscious Self. Embodied healing recognizes the interconnectedness of your whole being.

Embodied healing is not about fixing or curing; it's about BELIEVING in the balance and healing of your core wounds be it sexual, emotional, physical, spiritual, ancestral, and/or environmental.

As you see with neuroplasticity, the power to heal yourself literally comes from within. Embodied healing is the integration of your healing and its lessons while tapping into your internal resources of capacity, capability, desirability to find and/or return to balance, peace, and well-being. Neuroscience research by Dr. Joe Dispenza shows a person becomes the healing they desire by having both a coherent in both mind (6th and 7th energy centers) and heart (4th energy center). Coherent means to be a unified whole. This means you must be aligned with your Self. Activating your internal resources, in addition to, the alignment of your mind and your heart which requires the healing vibrations of emotions of faith, hope, confidence with the skill of discernment, you will literally become your own liberator, a self-liberator. You will be able to free yourself from self-limiting beliefs that fill you with self-doubt. This is embodied healing. As an embodied healer and self-liberator, your self-worth, self-esteem, and self-confidence will become reconnected with your body, mind, and spirit and listening to your intuition and their wisdom.

As a self-liberator, you take charge of your own healing process. You can explore different practices and healing strategies that resonate with you, whether it's meditation, mindful movement, energy work, life coaching and/or therapy. You learn to listen to your body's signals and honor your emotions. You embrace self-care to nurture and support yourself. Through embodied healing, you become the author of your own story, your healing narrative. You discover the power within you to transform, grow, and find a deep sense of well-being. It's a journey of self-discovery, self-empowerment, and ultimately, self-liberation. *Before you SHIFT your healing: Let's talk about your CAPE...*

Your C.A.P.E.: Being Present and Sustaining the Liberating Fruit of Self-Care

In the pursuit of making a difference in your world, you often find yourself tirelessly striving to save others, to bring about positive change, and to make an impact. But in this noble endeavor, you must pause and reflect: Is there any cape left to save yourself with the same cape you are using to save others? You will not be able to sustain the healing insights, lessons, tools and skills, connection to your relationship to healing if you do not reflect on your relationship to your current embodiment. For this self-assessment, use the acronym *C.A.P.E.*

C stands for Capacity

Capacity is your emotional and mental availability which creates the space of presence and your ability to create change and navigate life's ebbs and flows. To assess your capacity, explore your emotional and mental well-being and safety.

Scale the availability using 0-10 with 0 as no availability and 10 as full availability. Having capacity allows you to make choices that will prevent self-sacrifice.

A stands for Awareness: The Act of Being Present

To be in relationship with your body is to be present-- to be consciously aware of your interactions of your emotions, thoughts, and behaviors. Awareness is the key to being present. Being present unlocks the door to self-care and self-liberation. By cultivating mindfulness and being fully aware in the present moment, you deepen your connection with yourself, your surroundings, and the impact of The Defaults. Through awareness, you tune in to your core wounds, your core needs, and your core desires. This leads to engaging in self-permission and grounded and intuitive decision-making.

P represents Perspective: Whose Measuring Stick Are You Using?

Perspective is the lens through which you view yourselves and the world. It is crucial to question whose societal and sexual values, assumptions and expectations or measuring stick you are using when evaluating your intentions and choices. Are you internalizing society's assumptions and expectations, or are you defining your own? By cultivating a perspective grounded in self-compassion and authenticity, you free yourself from the pressure of external judgments and embrace a sense of authenticity and self-acceptance.

E denotes Expectation: Unpacking Self-Expectations

Expectations you place on yourselves can either propel you forward or become burdens that hinder your growth. Wounds like hyper-independence, perfectionism and self-doubt require significant unpacking and unlearning. By examining and reevaluating your expectations, you create space for flexibility, growth, and self-compassion. It is through releasing unrealistic expectations that you open yourself to the freedom of transformation and healing.

As you center yourself, nurturing your self-awareness and well-being, you embark on a transformative journey. You learn to wield your cape of saving your Self with care and intention.

So, center yourself amidst the chaos, grounding yourself in awareness, perspective, and the liberation of releasing self-limiting beliefs and self-imposed expectations. In doing so, you honor your own well-being and empower yourself to make a difference that is sustainable, authentic, and driven by the truest version of who you are.

Faith, Hope, Confidence, & Discernment: Spirituality & The Liberating Act of Choosing Your WHOLE- Self

What is Spirituality?

At its core, ***spirituality is the process of raising one's consciousness and aligning with higher states of connection to self, others, divinity, divine purpose, and self-understanding***. It often involves releasing old patterns, healing past wounds, and stepping into a more expansive sense of self. A ***spiritual awakening*** bridges the gap between survival-based living and a more intentional, thriving existence.

Symptoms of Spiritual Awakening

As one begins to become energetically aligned and spiritually awaken, certain symptoms may arise as the mind, body, and spirit adjust to this new state of being. These may include:

- **Physical symptoms**: Fatigue, changes in appetite, or unexplained aches and pains as the body adjusts to higher vibrations.

- **Emotional fluctuations**: Heightened sensitivity, sudden mood swings, or intense feelings of joy or sadness.

- **Mental clarity**: Increased awareness of thought patterns and a desire to break free from limiting beliefs.

- **Spiritual sensitivity**: Feeling more connected to nature, experiencing vivid dreams, or sensing energy shifts around you.

- **Sexual Desire Changes:** Your desire to have sex changes. You may not be attracted to your current lover(s), desire emotional connection or other intimacy needs to experience sexual desire, and you may experience highs and lows in your desire to have sex.

These symptoms are part of the process of moving beyond survival and creating a life rooted in thriving.

Thrivorship: The Embodied Wellness Connection to Spirituality

Thrivorship is the state of moving from merely getting through life to embracing a life of meaning, joy, and well-being. Embodied wellness is essential for thrivorship because it is ***knowing and believing in the healing of your mind, body, and spirit as one cohesive system.*** My experience and the research in sexual well-being and wellness show that having an affirming relationship to spirit and Spirit is a huge part of our ability to thrive. After 23 years of being a trauma-responsive integrative somatic psychotherapist, an embodied wellness coach, and almost 10 of those years as a clinical somatic sexologist, I created an embodied liberation healing path, Healing the Erotic Self (HTES). From my years in both my personal healing practices & my professional practices, I was frustrated to only be " Other Considerations" in academia and its literature as a Black woman or in community spaces as a spiritual queer person without a seemingly accessible or liberating path to develop routines, strategies, or coaching with healing practices that affirmed me nor my clients' WHOLE-Self ancestrally, somatically, culturally, sexually, energetically, and spiritually- our erotic wholeness.

Erotic wholeness is honored as a birthright, and liberation is embodied through somatic, spiritual, and ancestral healing practices that affirm our humanity, our joy, and our pleasure. SHIFT is part of the HTES Erotic Liberation Ecosystem to help survivors and healing professionals create embodied safety and self-trust. Healing The Erotic Self was created to help us navigate our relationship between our sexuality and our spirituality. The four part mind-body healing framework, SHIFT, helps you regulate your emotions, dissolve negative self-talk, and create safety within your body and empower your relationship to your intuition & self-trust —one breath, one intention, one choice, & one presence practice at a time. SHIFT introduces you to the erospiritual approach that is Healing the Erotic Self. So, what is Erospirituality? First, let's look at the core elements of spirituality.

The core elements of spirituality include:

1. **Connection** – to the self, others, nature, ancestors, or the divine

2. **Meaning-making** – asking questions like "Why am I here?" or "What is my purpose?"

3. **Inner experience** – a felt sense of peace, awe, or alignment

4. **Practice** – rituals or habits like meditation, prayer, breathwork, or service that deepen presence and awareness

5. **Values-based living** – aligning actions with core values like compassion, justice, love, and integrity

When you integrate spirituality into your sexual wellness journey, healing becomes erotic as it embraces a wholeness approach to healing. Spiritual practices incorporating the erotic such as erotic energy work, erotic mindfulness, and erotic breathwork invite you to attune to your erotic self. This connection helps dissolve sexually related distress and fosters an erotic resilience that creates an affirming capacity for emotional and physical ability to experience sexual pleasure without the sexual distress of shame, guilt, or distress.

Healing becomes a sacred practice when you:

- **Acknowledge pain:** Recognize your erotic wounds without judgment.

- **Surrender survival mode:** Compassionately acknowledge and replace fight, flight, freeze, and fawn responses.

- **Embrace your worth:** Realize and believe you deserve a joyful, pleasurable, and thriving life.

- **Intentional Impact:** Create healing practices like erotic energy work to create transformational healing.

- **Energy work is a powerful way to align with your ascension journey.** Practices like Self-Reiki, Emotional Freedom Technique (EFT), Erotic Breathwork, and/or SHIFT Somatic Healing Practice allow you to work with the body's energetic systems to release blockages and restore harmony.

Energy Work as Spirituality

Energy work isn't just a wellness tool—it's a spiritual practice. When you work with energy, you tap into the universal life force, often referred to as chi, prana, KA, or spirit. By addressing the energy flow within, you honor the sacredness of your body and spirit.

Erospirituality is the sacred fusion of sexuality, spirituality, and the intuitive relationship between mind, body, and energy. This eros becomes a grounding force that roots you in truth and liberates you from "the Defaults", oppressive societal and sexual norms.

As an erotic intelligence practice, *Erospirituality* reclaims the erotic self as a daily source of power rather than a shadow of shame. Erospirituality is the care of your lovership.

In this liberating work, Healing the Erotic Self blends ***sexuality, spirituality, and mind-body healing***

with a decolonial understanding of eroticism, thus decolonizing the erotic not just as sexual energy, but as a *spiritual energy*—a source of inner power, empowered embodiment, collective connection, and liberation. Spirituality, in this sense, is a healing relationship with one's whole self, including the erotic.

***Eroticism as spirituality is Erospirituality,
the methodology to erotic liberation.***

Developing Your Spiritual Presence Practice

A thriving ascension practice requires self-awareness, intention, and consistent effort. Here's how to begin:

1. Cultivate Self-*Awareness*

- Journal daily to explore your emotions, thoughts, and behaviors.

- Notice patterns that no longer serve your well-being.

- Spend quiet time in reflection to connect with your intuition.

2. Set *Intentions*

- Define what thriving looks like for you.

- Create affirmations that support your ascension journey.

- Focus your energy on what aligns with your highest self.

3. Make the *Effort*

- Commit to daily, weekly, monthly, quarterly, and yearly spiritual practices.

- Prioritize rest and restoration to support your energetic body and spirit, or the conscious awareness of your energy body.

- Seek guidance from somatic and spiritual healers, erosomatic coaches, somatic sexologists, somatic therapists, or mentors who align with your path.

From Surviving to Thriving

Transitioning from survival to thriving requires a holistic approach that combines embodied wellness, spirituality, and energy work. By cultivating self-awareness, setting clear intentions, and making consistent efforts, you can create a spiritual practice that supports your growth, healing, and ultimate flourishing.

Embodied wellness is not a destination; it's a journey—a practice of living fully and authentically. This week focuses on how to use eroticism and your erotic energy as a spiritual practice.

REFLECTION QUESTIONS:

1. When do I feel most connected to something greater than myself?

2. How do I practice spirituality in my daily life?

3. What values or experiences matter most to my spiritual path?

4. In what ways does my spirituality support my healing and erotic embodiment?

5. How do I define spiritual alignment for myself?

6. What practices or rituals help me feel spiritually grounded?

7. How does my spiritual path relate to my cultural or ancestral identity?

____

____

____

____

____

Reconnecting to Your Spirit

As you have learned by reading this book, when I am referring to spirit, I am not referring to Spirit as in religious dogma. I am referring to spirit as in the relationship between your conscious awareness, your energy, and your intuition. I am closing this guide by offering you another personal story of how much I believe in your healing, our collective healing, and how SHIFT can literally be lifesaving. This level of vulnerability is being shared because I have come to feel safe enough to share only in my teaching environment-professional use of the self.

Here it goes....

August 2020 I was in a place that the thoughts of my daughter and grandbaby could not bring me back from. I was tired. Prior to the beginning of the pandemic, I had experienced some catastrophic events. As I was experiencing business and economic failure, I felt shame and guilt. I also felt unsupported when I saw how others personally blamed me for things that were systematically out of my control. It's not easy to not care what others say or do when it impacts one's livelihood. At that point, I was in my healing where finding & losing courage was devastating.

I called my daughter and shared my despair, and she said, "Mom, you have two choices. You either lean back into your healing or you are going to a hospital."

I didn't want to lose that fight so I chose (am choosing) to live. I choose me- an abundant me, a me that is not valued by professional achievements, social or economic class but rather an abundant me that is rooted in safety and self-liberation.

My healing, my increased visibility, and the things seen as my professional self is not a gimmick. I believe WHOLEHEARTEDLY in the power of healing. I chose to return to my healing practice with a deliberate intention of living WELL. It's me choosing to live. SHIFT allowed me to decolonize somatics and decolonize healing by reclaiming sexuality, somatics, and spirituality through erotic intelligence, integrative somatic healing, decolonial spirituality with trauma-informed healing practices rooted in the ancestral wisdom of the Global Majority of Black, Caribbean, African, Indigenous Turtle Islanders, Latine, East Asian, South Asian, and Pacific cultures.

From then to now, it has been 3 years since I decided to survive active suicidal ideation. I have used SHIFT in combination of plant medicine, hypnotherapy, erotic hypnotherapy, energy healing, breathwork, mindful movement and erotic coaching. In my healing, I recognized there were other internal resources I briefly mentioned earlier that I was not familiar with and could only develop a relationship to them by sustaining my healing.

Those internal resources that moved me from surviving to thriving were:

- Faith is confidence in what we hope for and assurance about what we do not see.
- Hope is a feeling of expectation and desire for what you want to happen.
- Confidence is the ability to believe in oneself.
- Discernment is the ability to judge well.
- You don't have to be strong, be committed. Be willing to commit to your WHOLE-Self & your healing.
- Call back your energy and internal resources and choose yourself. SHIFT your healing.

I want to thank my daughter who, along with myself, is absolutely my best friend. Her belief in my healing is what evolved our parent-child relationship into a healing kinship. I have activated and remain in my healing, committed every day to myself, my care, and my living. At the time I wrote this book, I was a digital nomad and traveling healing professional living between the Dominican Republic and Delaware, coaching and curating healing spaces, supporting clients in their post-traumatic growth and healing.

"Caring for myself is not self-indulgence.

It is self-preservation and that is an act of political warfare."

-Audre Lorde

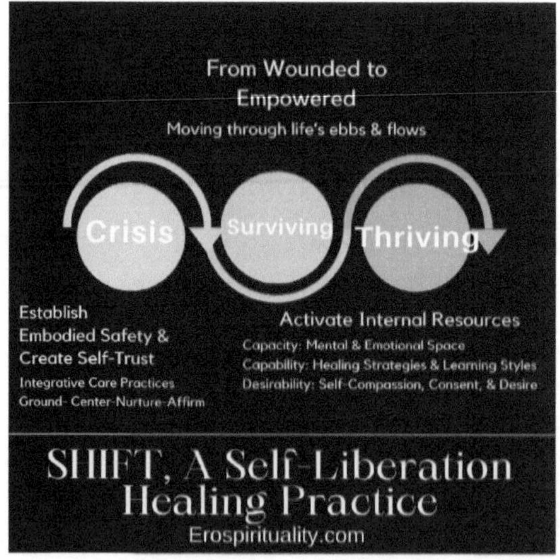

CHAPTER 8

SHIFT, A Self-Liberation

Healing Practice

Witness Your Emotions

Cultivate Your Mind

Nurture Your Body

Connect to Your Spirit

Cleanse, Protect, & Replenish Your Energy

Embody Your Healing

Activate Your Presence Practice

Actualize your WHOLENESS

SHIFT: Moving from Wounded to Empowered,

A Self-Liberation Healing Practice

Care Practice 1: Ground (Your Self) -Connecting to **Presence in a Distressed Moment**

With this initial care, you recognize that you are experiencing distress and/or witnessing intense emotions. You recognize you are not feeling safe and understand the importance of being present to create safety. By grounding yourself in the present moment, you begin by cultivating a sense of awareness through the practice of mindfulness and conscious breathing. You don't have to fix or solve anything. You just have to connect safely to this moment. By attuning yourself to be present in the here and now, you establish your commitment for self-liberation and transformation. You are actively choosing a new path, a healing path.

Care Practice 2: Center (Your Self)- Getting Clarity **by Centering Your WHOLE-Self**

With this care practice, you recognize the relationship between your identity and your power (agency and autonomy). You fight the pull to use your C.A.P.E. in ways that are self-sacrificing. With the healing strategy of using clarifying questions, you become clear on what is in your best interest. By asking yourself clarifying questions, you examine the purpose and intention of the distressful moment you are in. . By centering yourself with your radical honesty and authenticity, you prioritize your core needs and your core desires from a place you're using your measuring stick or values. By centering yourself. you reclaim our power and navigate life with intentionality and clarity.

Care Practice 3: Nurture (Your Self) - Activating Self-Compassion

With Care Practice 3, you begin to explore your use of self-compassion in action with healing practice and routines you have self-identified as care practices that bring you a sense of safety, joy, and/or comfort. By nurturing yourself, you begin to explore your relationship with self-limiting beliefs, your energy, your intuition, and your spirit and how your mind and body inform your relationship to self-esteem, self-worth, and self-confidence. By focusing on your locust of control of your beliefs, mindset, and behaviors, you develop a relationship to self-care practices that become a lifestyle of liberated living. With my clients, I often encourage reclaiming healing practices informed by your culture and ancestry. By nurturing yourself, you dissolve shame and self-doubt and move into a place of becoming self-assured.

Care Practice 4: Affirm (Your Self) - Reinforcing Self-Compassion & Self-Liberation

With this care practice, you focus on reframing negative thoughts and self-limiting beliefs with words of affirmation and empowering self-talk. You identify positive beliefs and phrases of encouragement that resonate with you thus reinforcing your self-worth, self-esteem, self-confidence, with the authenticity and self-compassion you exercised by completing any or all of the preceding Care Practices 1-3. By consciously choosing affirmations that acknowledge your capacity, capabilities, and desires, you develop and reinforce a liberating mindset and embodiment cultivating and sustaining a loving relationship with yourself.

Note: Depending on the intensity of the distress you are experiencing you may use one, some of all of the SHIFT Care Practices to establish safety and create trust within your WHOLE-Self.

Exercise: Creating Affirmations

As a hypnotherapist, I have learned the formula of creating empowering affirmations that your mind and body will believe and embody. First and foremost, without belief, you will not be able to activate the affirmation. Believe or have hope in the affirmation you are creating. An embodied belief is a value-informed statement in which your mind, body, and spirit aligns with.

Now, here are two things you need to include when you are creating an affirmation- your presence and your intention.

Healing Formula

Affirmation= PRESENCE + INTENTION

As part of Care Practice 4: Affirm, here are the following affirmation suggestions to inspire and support your journey:

1. *"I am capable."* Affirm your inherent ability to navigate challenges, learn, and grow. Recognize that you possess the strength and skills to overcome obstacles and create positive change in your life.

2. *"I am worthy."* Affirm your intrinsic worthiness. Embrace the understanding that you are deserving of love, respect, and happiness. Recognize that your worthiness is not determined by external validation but resides within you, unconditionally.

Through SHIFT, A Self-Liberation Practice, you embark on a safe and sustained healing journey. By grounding yourself, centering your core wounds, core needs and core desires in addition to, nurturing your WHOLE-Self, and affirming your embodiment, you move from a place of woundedness to empowerment. This self-liberation healing practice empowers you to embrace your most authentic self, cultivate self-compassion and self-trust, and live an intuitive and liberated life.

Now that we have covered what informs this healing practice and what you can expect by engaging and incorporating this healing practice into your everyday life, the following pages give a guide on how to implement SHIFT as a self-liberation healing practice. SHIFT will complement most healing practices such as therapy, life coaching, and is not meant to be used in place of therapy or medical intervention.

If you are experiencing a mental health crisis 988, message HOME or HOLA on WhatsApp the Crisis Text Line at 741741

Taking care of yourself is not always easy to do. Growing and maturing does not just happen physically. As you are aware, it also happens emotionally and mentally. You are developing inside and out. Developing a safe and trusting relationship with yourself requires you to learn the skills of self-awareness, self-soothing, and self-regulation. Now that you can understand how your emotions is energy in motion that you feel as physical or bodily sensations, in addition to, emotional and trauma responses, learning to take care of yourself with care practices that support your nervous system is very important to your overall development. Below are some strategies to help you learn how to develop a more confident and trusting relationship with yourself. To get the SHIFT Meditation and Wellness Plan, visit SHIFTHealing.co. Use code- SHIFTBOOK.

SHIFT: A Self-Liberation Practice, Healing Framework, & System of Self-Care

SHIFT Care Practice: Ground

1. Focus (Activate Your Presence Practice)
a. Witnessed Emotion: Pay attention to your first awareness of being in distress or feeling uncomfortable. Activate your presence practice.

2. Breathe

a. Take the Sacred Pause of 3 full belly breaths. (inhale 5 count-no hold-exhale 5 count)

3. Practice Your Presence Practice w/ Mindfulness
a. Scale from 0-10 the intensity of your witnessed emotion.

SHIFT Care Practice: Center
Activate self-compassion.
Pick one, more, or all of the following processing questions to
manage your distress and/or discomfort and center yourself for your highest and greatest good:

- How do I take care of myself in this moment?
- What is in your best interest?
- What is the purpose of this interaction?
- What is the witnessed emotion telling me about myself?

SHIFT Care Practice: Nurture

Activate self-permission to be present.
List 5 self-soothing activities to practice for 10-15 minutes to
create safety & support you in decreasing the intensity of your witnessed emotions and/or distress.

1. Hear 2. Smell 3. Vision 4. Touch

5. Taste 6. Intutition

SHIFT Care Practice: Affirm

Challenge your negative self-talk with words of encouragement, self-compassion, gentleness, and self-acceptance.
Answer the following:
What positive belief or words/phrase of encouragement resonates with you?

What will verbally reinforce the self-love and Self-compassion you just provided yourself?

Affirmation suggestions:

1)I am empowered.   2) I am worthy.   3) I am desirable.
4) I am safe.   5) I am divine.

SHIFT Care Practice I: Ground

1.Focus (**Activate Your Presence Practice**)

a. Witnessed Emotion: Pay attention to your first awareness of being in distress

or feeling uncomfortable. Activate your presence practice.

2.**Breathe**

a. Take the Sacred Pause of 3 full belly breaths. (inhale 5 count-no hold-exhale 5 count)

3.**Practice Your Presence Practice w/ Mindfulness**

a. Scale from 0-10 the intensity of your witnessed emotion.

Integration Practice Self-Reflection:

____

____

____

____

____

____

____

____

____

SHIFT Care Practice II: Center

Activate self-compassion. Pick one, more, or all of the following processing questions to

manage your distress and/or discomfort and center yourself for your highest and greatest good:

•How do I take care of myself in this moment?

•What is in your best interest?

•What is the purpose of this interaction?

•What is the witnessed emotion telling me about myself?

Integration Practice Self-Reflection:

____

____

____

____

____

____

____

____

____

____

____

SHIFT Care Practice III: Nurture

Activate self-permission to be present: List 5 self-soothing activities to practice from 10-15 minutes

to create safety & support you in decreasing the intensity of your witnessed emotions and/or distress.

1. Hear:

2. Smell:

3. Vision:

4. Touch:

5. Taste:

6. Intuition:

Integration Practice Self-Reflection:

____

____

____

____

____

____

____

____

SHIFT Care Practice IV: Affirm

Challenge your negative self-talk with words of encouragement, self-compassion, gentleness, and self-acceptance.

Answer the following:

What positive belief or words/phrase of encouragement resonates with you?

•What will verbally reinforce the self-love and Self-compassion you just provided yourself?

Affirmation suggestions:

1) I am empowered.

2) I am worthy.

3) I am desirable.

4) I am safe.

 5) I am divine.

Integration Practice Self-Reflection:

____

____

____

____

____

Self and Emotional Regulation Care Practices

1) Top-Down Strategies for Nervous System Regulation

    a. Refers to strengthening the body's response to body sensations.

    b. Recommended Care Practices:

        i. Meditation

        ii. Yoga

        iii. Journaling/Self-Reflection

        iv. Affirmation Practice

        v. Aromatherapy

2) Bottom-Up Strategies for Nervous System Regulation

    a. Refers to resetting the automatic nervous system (ANS) to a state of rest.

    b. Automatic nervous system regulates the body functions of the heart, lungs, stomach, and reproductive organs.

c. **R**ecommended Care Practices

    i. Breathwork

    ii. Mindful Moment

    iii. Consensual Touch (Attachment and Attunement)

        1. Massage & Self-Massage

        2. Reiki

        3. Holding hands

        4. Hugs

        5. Cuddles

        6. Weighted blanket

Using the affirmation healing formula given earlier, create your own healing affirmations for each energy center:

1st Energy Center- Safety and Stability

I am____

____

I am____

____

2nd Energy Center- Creativity & Desirability

I desire____

____

I create____

____

3rd Energy Center- Connection, Confidence, Intuition

I honor____

____

I trust____

____

4th Energy Center- Love, Hope, Self-Worth, Optimism

I love____

____

I love____

____

5th Energy Center-- Truth and Communication

My truth____

____

My voice____

____

6th Energy Center- Self-Awareness & Discernment

I see____

____

I know____

____

7th Energy Healing- Self as Source, Self-Assured, Divinity

I understand

____

____

The SHIFT Meditation: Balancing Your Energy Centers

In this meditation practice, we will focus on shifting and balancing your energy centers using diaphragmatic breathing and the visualization of a golden light. This meditation will help you ground, center, nurture, and affirm each energy center for a harmonious flow of energy throughout your body.

Preparation:

- Find a quiet and comfortable place to sit or lie down. Ensure that you won't be disturbed during your meditation.

- Take a few deep breaths to relax your body and mind. Inhale deeply through your nose, letting your abdomen rise, and exhale slowly through your mouth, letting go of any tension.

- Close your eyes and bring your attention to your breath. Begin to breathe deeply and rhythmically, focusing on each breath as it enters and leaves your body.

Step 1: Grounding - Root Chakra

- Visualize a vibrant, glowing red energy center at the base of your spine. This is your Root Chakra.

- As you inhale, imagine a golden light descending from above, filling your Root Chakra with warmth and vitality.

- As you exhale, envision any tension or negativity leaving your Root Chakra and dissipating into the earth below.

- Affirmation: "I am grounded and secure. I am connected to the Earth's energy."

Step 2: Centering - Sacral Chakra

- Move your attention to the area just below your navel, visualizing a beautiful orange energy center, your Sacral Chakra.

- Inhale deeply, allowing a golden light to flow into your Sacral Chakra, rejuvenating and balancing it.

- As you exhale, release any emotional blockages or stress from this energy center.

- Affirmation: "I embrace my creativity and passion. I am in tune with my emotions."

Step 3: Nurturing - Solar Plexus Chakra

- Shift your focus to the area above your navel, where you can see a bright yellow energy center, your Solar Plexus Chakra.

- Inhale, and imagine a warm, golden light filling your Solar Plexus Chakra, nourishing it with confidence and empowerment.

- As you exhale, release any self-doubt or insecurity from this energy center.

- Affirmation: "I am confident and strong. I trust in my inner power."

Step 4: Affirmation - Heart Chakra

- Bring your attention to your heart area, visualizing a radiant green energy center, your Heart Chakra.

- Inhale deeply, allowing a golden light to envelop and heal your Heart Chakra with love and compassion.

- As you exhale, release any pain or hurt, forgiving and letting go of any negativity.

- Affirmation: "I love and accept myself. I am open to giving and receiving love."

Step 5: Affirmation - Throat Chakra

- Move your awareness to your throat, seeing a brilliant blue energy center, your Throat Chakra.

- Inhale, and visualize a golden light filling your Throat Chakra, helping you express yourself authentically.

- As you exhale, release any fear or hesitation, allowing your voice to flow freely.

- Affirmation: "I speak my truth with clarity and kindness. My voice matters."

Step 6: Affirmation - Third Eye Chakra

- Focus on the space between your eyebrows, envisioning an indigo energy center, your Third Eye Chakra.

- Inhale deeply, inviting a golden light to illuminate your Third Eye Chakra, enhancing your intuition and insight.

- As you exhale, let go of any doubts or illusions that may cloud your perception.

- Affirmation: "I trust my inner wisdom. I see the truth in all things."

Step 7: Affirmation - Crown Chakra

- Finally, direct your attention to the top of your head, picturing a radiant violet energy center, your Crown Chakra.

- Inhale, and imagine a golden light descending into your Crown Chakra, connecting you to the universal energy.

- As you exhale, release any attachments or limitations, opening yourself to higher consciousness.

- Affirmation: "I am one with the universe. I am divinely guided and protected."

Conclusion:

Take a few moments to breathe deeply and bask in the harmonious glow of your balanced energy centers. When you are ready, gently open your eyes and carry this sense of balance and alignment with you throughout your day.

Practice this SHIFT meditation regularly to maintain a healthy flow of energy and promote emotional, mental, and physical well-being.

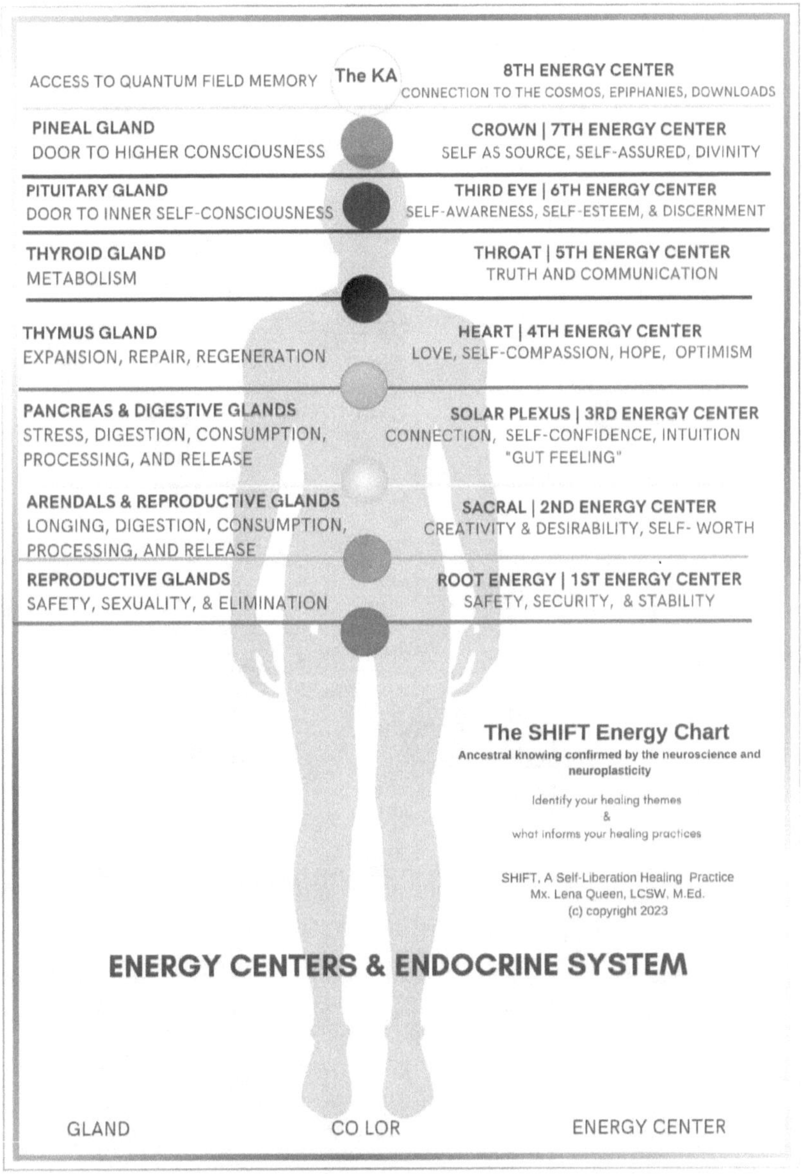

ACCESS TO QUANTUM FIELD MEMORY
The KA
8TH ENERGY CENTER
CONNECTION TO THE COSMOS, EPIPHANIES, DOWNLOADS
PINEAL GLAND
DOOR TO HIGHER CONSCIOUSNESS
CROWN | 7TH ENERGY CENTER
SELF AS SOURCE, SELF-ASSURED, DIVINITY
PITUITARY GLAND
DOOR TO INNER SELF-CONSCIOUSNESS
THIRD EYE | 6TH ENERGY CENTER
SELF-AWARENESS, SELF-ESTEEM, & DISCERNMENT
THYROID GLAND
METABOLISM
THROAT | 5TH ENERGY CENTER
TRUTH AND COMMUNICATION
THYMUS GLAND
EXPANSION, REPAIR, REGENERATION
HEART | 4TH ENERGY CENTER
LOVE, SELF-COMPASSION, HOPE, OPTIMISM
PANCREAS & DIGESTIVE GLANDS
STRESS, DIGESTION, CONSUMPTION, PROCESSING, AND RELEASE
SOLAR PLEXUS | 3RD ENERGY CENTER
CONNECTION, SELF-CONFIDENCE, INTUITION "GUT FEELING"
ARENDALS & REPRODUCTIVE GLANDS
LONGING, DIGESTION, CONSUMPTION, PROCESSING, AND RELEASE
SACRAL | 2ND ENERGY CENTER
CREATIVITY & DESIRABILITY, SELF- WORTH
REPRODUCTIVE GLANDS
SAFETY, SEXUALITY, & ELIMINATION
ROOT ENERGY | 1ST ENERGY CENTER
SAFETY, SECURITY, & STABILITY
The SHIFT Energy Chart
Ancestral knowing confirmed by the neuroscience and neuroplasticity
Identify your healing themes
&
what informs your healing practices
SHIFT, A Self-Liberation Healing Practice
Mx. Lena Queen, LCSW, M.Ed.
(c) copyright 2023
ENERGY CENTERS & ENDOCRINE SYSTEM
GLAND
CO LOR
ENERGY CENTER

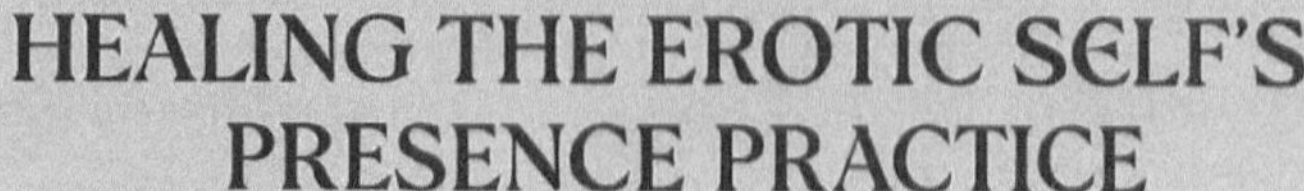

YOUR PRESENCE PRACTICE

TO MANAGE

MINDSET

MOODS

MOVEMENTS

- DECISION-MAKING
- PROTECTIVE PATTERNS

AWARENESS

INTENTION

Conscious thinking

EFFORT

Stream of *consciousness*

Subscious beliefs

With your permission, allow me to remind you:
You are a lover, and you are already WHOLE.
This presence practice and intentionality is your
erotic self-awareness—what I call *lovership*. The
embodiment of your lovership is called *The Erotic Sef*.

Erospirituality.com

#Eroticintelligence #HealingTheEroticSelf #SomaticHealing #Erospi-

In My Healing: My SHIFT Care Plan

I. *Ground: Establish Safety and Stay Present*
- Take the Sacred Pause of 3 full belly breaths

  Core Wounds: Self-Worth, Self-Esteem, and/or Self-Confidence

- What's the Witnessed Emotion(s):_______________________

- Where do you feel it in your body:

  ____

- What age do you feel:

  ____

II. *Center: Get Clear & Create Your Intentions*
- Process SHIFT's Clarifying Questions (See Chart)

- Name Your Self-Limiting Beliefs:

  ____

- Healing Theme via Energy Center (See SHIFT Energy Chart):_______________________

  ____

- Shadow Work (Self-Sabotaging Behavior to Address):

  ____

III. Nurture: Your Care Practices to Establish Safety &
Develop an Intuitive Self-Trust

- **Mind (Meditation):**

  ____

- **Body (Mindful Movement):**

  ____

- **Spirit (Energy Practice):**

  ____

IV. Affirm: Create an Empowering Belief of Your Self

- **My Empowered Belief:**

  ____

SHIFT *Integration Practice: A Moment of Self-Reflection*

Who are you without the impact of that core wound? Who are you in your healing?

In My Healing: My SHIFT Care Plan

I. Ground: Establish Safety and Stay Present

- Take the Sacred Pause of 3 full belly breaths

- Core Wounds:

  Self-Worth, Self-Esteem, and/or Self-Confidence

- What's the Witnessed
  Emotion(s):__________________________________

  - Where do you feel it in your body:

    ____

  - What age do you feel:

    ____

II. Center: Get Clear & Create Your Intentions

- Process SHIFT's Clarifying Questions (See Chart)

- Name Your Self-Limiting Beliefs:

  ____

- Healing Theme via Energy Center (See SHIFT Energy
  Chart):

  ____

- Shadow Work (Self-Sabotaging Behavior to Address):

  ____

III. *Nurture: Your Care Practices to Establish Safety & Develop an Intuitive Self-Trust*

- •Mind (Meditation):

____

- Body (Mindful Movement):

____

- Spirit (Energy Practice):

____

IV. *Affirm: Create an Empowering Belief of Your Self*

- My Empowered Belief:

____

SHIFT *Integration Practice:*
A Moment of Self-Reflection

Who are you be without the impact of that core wound?
Who are you in your healing?

Erosomatics: Erotic Care Practices for Sexual and WHOLE-Self Healing

Here are three erosomatic practices to support sexual healing through the integration of neuroplasticity and the Polyvagal Theory:

1. Breath & Body Awareness (Neurorelaxation)

How: Begin by lying down in a safe, comfortable space. Place one hand on your chest and one on your belly. Practice slow, deep breathing, allowing yourself to feel the rise and fall of your breath. Notice any areas of tension or numbness in your body, and breathe into those spaces.

Why: This practice helps activate the ventral vagal state, signaling safety and presence to the nervous system. By fostering relaxation and awareness, you reduce the tendency to dissociate during intimate moments.

2. Sensual Self-Touch (Neurostimulation)

How: Explore self-touch in a way that feels nurturing and non-goal-oriented. Use different textures (such as silk, feathers, or warm oil) and sensations (light strokes, firmer pressure) to reconnect with your body's capacity for pleasure. Stay present with the sensations, rather than focusing on sexual performance.

Why: This practice stimulates neural pathways associated with pleasure, creating positive associations between touch and safety. It helps move your body from a sympathetic or dorsal vagal state into a more relaxed, pleasure-oriented ventral vagal state.

3. Erotic Movement Practice (Sequencing & Neurorepair)

How: Choose a piece of music that makes you feel safe and open. Allow your body to move however it wants, paying attention to where you hold tension or where you feel more free. This movement can be as small as a hand gesture or as expansive as full-body dancing.

Why: Movement can unlock stored trauma in the body, releasing shame or discomfort around sexual expression. This practice gradually rewires the brain and body to associate movement and expression with pleasure and safety, following the principles of neurorepair.

EFT Tapping Practice for Increased Self-Confidence and Feeling Desirable

Step 1: Preparation

Reflect on how confident and desirable you currently feel. Rate this on a scale of 0-10 (10 being the highest level of confidence and desirability). Identify any limiting beliefs or emotions, such as "I'm not good enough" or "I don't feel attractive."

Step 2: Tapping Script

Setup Statement (Karate Chop Point):

While tapping on the karate chop point, repeat three times:

"Even though I don't always feel confident or desirable, I deeply and completely accept myself just as I am."

"Even though I sometimes doubt my worth and attractiveness, I choose to honor myself and my journey."

"Even though I struggle with self-confidence, I am ready to release these doubts and embrace my innate beauty and power."

Tapping Sequence for Releasing Self-Doubt:

Tap on the following points while repeating the phrases:

- **Eyebrow Point:** "I don't feel confident or desirable right now."

- **Side of Eye:** "I doubt my worth and my attractiveness."

- **Under Eye:** "I feel insecure and unsure about myself."

- **Under Nose:** "It's hard to see my own beauty and power."

- **Chin Point:** "I compare myself to others and feel less than."

- **Collarbone:** "These doubts make me feel small and unseen."

- **Under Arm:** "I carry the fear that I'm not enough."

- **Top of Head:** "I'm ready to release these limiting beliefs about myself."

<u>Tapping Sequence for Releasing Negative Beliefs:</u>

Continue tapping through the points:

- **Eyebrow Point:** "What if I'm more than enough, just as I am?"

- **Side of Eye:** "I release the belief that I need to be perfect to feel desirable."

- **Under Eye:** "I let go of the fear that I'm not attractive or worthy."

- **Under Nose:** "I release the need for external validation."

- **Chin Point:** "I choose to see myself with love and compassion."

- **Collarbone:** "I forgive myself for believing I'm not enough."

- **Under Arm:** "I let go of self-doubt and embrace my unique beauty."

- **Top of Head:** "I am free to feel confident and desirable in my own skin."

<u>Tapping Sequence for Building Confidence and Desirability:</u>

Tap through the points with positive affirmations:

Eyebrow Point: "I am radiant, confident, and desirable."

Side of Eye: "I embrace my unique beauty and power."

Under Eye: "I feel confident in my body and my energy."

Under Nose: "I am attractive just as I am right now."

Chin Point: "I radiate confidence and self-love."

Collarbone: "I feel magnetic, empowered, and desirable."

Under Arm: "I attract love and admiration by being authentically me."

Top of Head: "I am worthy of love, desire, and admiration."

Step 3: Integration

Take a deep breath, check in with yourself, and re-rate your confidence and desirability on a scale of 0-10. Notice any shifts in how you feel.

Step 4: Visualization (Optional)

After tapping, close your eyes and imagine yourself walking into a room exuding confidence and desirability. Picture others admiring your energy and presence. Feel the love and appreciation for yourself radiating outward.

Step 5: Daily Erotic Affirmations

Use the following affirmations to reinforce this practice:

"I am confident, radiant, and irresistible."

"I am proud of who I am, inside and out."

"I deserve to feel desirable and loved every day."

Neuroscience says it takes 66 days to create a new mindset and 15 minutes to self-regulate so let's combine **SHIFT** with this Ascension Practice for 66 days. If completing 66 consecutive days seems overwhelming, I recommend complete the Tapping Practice 2-4 times weekly for the next 8 weeks.

<u>SHIFT Liberated Living Structure & Strategies</u>
<u>Recommendations</u>

Recommended Practice Structure:
1. Prepare Body
   - Wash Face
   - Brush Teeth
   - Perfume (if desired)
2. Cleanse space with protection work

1.Rosemary or Bay Leaves, or Sea Salt Water Spray
3. Light Incense (Myrrh)
4. Light Candles
5. Express Gratitude
   - Give Honor to Creator, Ancestors, and Nature
   - Thank Universe for Self & Blessings, etc.
   - Give Statements of Gratitude
   - Can pour libations of water into a plant or ground as expressing gratitude.
6. Use Music, if desire
7. The Recommended Energy Practice (15-20 minutes)

8. Self-Reflection with Journaling, Voice Memo, or some other type of record keeping.
9. Cleansing Breath with the Sacred Pause
10. Move on with your day or night routine.

TIME OF PRACTICE

1. 6am - 8am Monday, Wednesday, Friday
2. 7am - 9am Tuesday, Thursday
3. 7am or 8am Saturday
4. 7am or 9am Sunday

Self-Reflection Notes:

____

____

____

____

____

____

____

____

____

<u>SHIFT Liberated Living Structure & Strategies</u> <u>Recommendations</u>

SHIFT MORNING RITUAL
1. Time Frame – 15 minutes to 2 hours; varies based on your time availability.
2. Daily Requirement

Sample SHIFT Morning Ritual
1. SHIFT Somatic Healing Meditation or Self-Reiki
2. Restorative Stretching
     a. Leg stretches and hip openers
     b. Cobra Pose
     c. Cat/Cow Pose
     d. Heaven Pose/Downward Dog
3. 3 Sun Salutations
4. Head Stand
5. Child Pose
6. Closing - State Affirmations while
7. Time Varies on pacing
8. 1 Full Breath with each pose/position and between movements
9. Complete session with #InMyHealing Erotic Affirmations Journal

SHIFT Somatic Healing Care Plan
for Embodied Healing

Morning:
1. Practice 5 minutes of breathing in the morning before you get out of bed.
2. Affirmation music
3. Take supplements daily. See recommendations below.

Mid-day Practice:
1. Restorative Breathwork with box breathing
2. Cannabidiol oil, or CBD
3. Sacred Pause Practice

Evening:
1. Stretching like Trauma-Release Poses or Restorative Yoga Movement
2. Affirmation Music
3. Chamomile Tea
4. 10-min Body Scan Meditation to prepare for sleep manage overthinking

Recommended Supplements:

1. Vitamin D (bone health and mental clarity)
2. Calcium Magnesium with Zinc (all in one pill; for mood regulation and cell repair)
3. B-Complex (mood, mental clarity, energy)
4. Omega 3-6-9 (brain fog, mental clarity, brain health)
5. Ginkgo Bilbao (for concentration and focus: take twice daily)
6. L-Theanine (amino acid for concentration and improved moods)
7. L-Tyrosine (an amino acid to build neurotransmitters for concentration and improved moods)
8. Lion's Mane mushroom (moods and mental clarity)
9. CBD Oil (mood management and sleep)
10. Chamomile Tea (Anxiety Support)
11. Chamomile and Lavender Tea (Anxiety and Sleep)
12. Oil of Oregano (3 drops) for immune system support.

Please research the recommended supplements and consult your doctor, especially if you are taking medication for any reason. Breathwork is the recommended somatic practice to help the client develop a mindful presence practice. For more somatic and Erosomatic practices and integration sessions, visit Erospirituality.com.

Aromatherapy

The National Association for Holistic Aromatherapy (NAHA) defines aromatherapy as "the therapeutic application or the medicinal use of aromatic substances (essential oils) for holistic healing." Aromatherapy, or essential oil therapy, refers to a range of traditional, alternative, or complementary therapies that use essential oils and other aromatic plant compounds. Essential oils have been used for nearly 6,000 years to improve a person's health or mood.

Benefits of aromatherapy to managing or reducing:

- Nausea
- Pain and body aches
- Anxiety, agitation, stress, and depression
- Fatigue and insomnia

- Muscular aches
- Headaches
- Circulatory problems
- Menstrual and/or Menopausal problems
- Alopecia, or hair loss

How to use aromatherapy:

Essential oils can be used for inhalation and topical use. Inhalation is smelling the fragrance of the essential oil to receive emotional and mental health benefits. Topical use involves applying the essential oil directly to your skin to reap the emotional, mental, and physical health benefits it offers.

Types of essential oils and their benefits

Basil essential oil is used to sharpen concentration and alleviate some of the symptoms of depression. It may relieve headaches and migraines. It should be avoided during pregnancy.

Bergamot essential oil is said to be helpful for the urinary and digestive tracts. When combined with eucalyptus oil, it may help relieve skin problems, including those caused by stress and chicken pox.

Rosemary essential oil may benefit the nervous and circulatory systems.

Black pepper essential oil is commonly used for stimulating circulation, relieving muscular aches and pains, and treating bruises. Combined with ginger essential oil, it is used to reduce arthritis pain and improve flexibility.

Chamomile essential oil can treat eczema and help calm anxiety.

Citronella essential oil is a relative of lemongrass and acts as an insect repellent.

Clove essential oil is a topical analgesic, or painkiller, that is commonly used for toothache. It is also used as an antispasmodic antiemetic, for preventing vomiting and nausea, and as a carminative, preventing gas in the gut. It has antimicrobial, antioxidant, and antifungal properties.

Eucalyptus essential oil can help relieve congestion in the airways during a cold or flu. It is often combined with peppermint. Many people are allergic to eucalyptus, so care should be taken.

Geranium essential oil can be used for skin problems, to reduce stress, and as a mosquito repellent.

Jasmine essential oil has been described as an aphrodisiac. While scientific evidence is lacking, research has shown that the odor of jasmine increases beta waves, which are linked to alertness.

Lavender essential oil is used as an antiseptic for minor cuts and burns and to enhance relaxation and sleep. It is said to relieve headache and migraine symptoms.

Lemon essential oil is said to improve mood and help relieve the symptoms of stress and depression.

Rosemary essential oil may promote hair growth, boost memory, prevent muscle spasms, and support the circulatory and nervous systems.

Some believe sandalwood essential oil to have aphrodisiac qualities.

Tea tree essential oil is said to have antimicrobial, antiseptic, and disinfectant qualities. It is commonly used in shampoos and skin care products to treat acne, burns, and bites. It is featured in mouth rinses, but it should never be swallowed, as it is toxic.

Thyme essential oil is said to help reduce fatigue, nervousness, and stress.

Yarrow essential oil is used to treat symptoms of cold and flu, and to help reduce joint inflammation.

Note: Essential Oils for a massage will be mixed with a topical or skin-safe oil such as Blackseed oil that dilutes the essential oil and provides lubrication.

Sound Healing Meditation Practices

Sounding healing is an ancient form of therapy that various cultures around the world have used for thousands of years. It involves the use of various sound frequencies and vibrations to promote healing, relaxation, and balance in the body, mind, and spirit. (Source: Quora.com)

Types of sound healing include- Singing Bowl, Gongs, Tuning Fork, Tuning fork therapy, Binaural beats, Chimes, Chanting DIY sound healing, Music therapy, Kalimba, Sound baths, Vibroacoustic therapy, Voice, Active sound therapy, Bonny Method, Brainwave entrainment, Didgeridoo, Drumming circle, Drums, Monochord, Rainstick, Tibetan Bowls, Meditating, and Music

Consider these frequencies when using sound healing as a self-care practice:

1) Morning Meditation
   a) Alpha Wave Meditation (8Hz| 13 Hz)
      i) Relaxation

ii) Abundant Thinking (Hope, Faith, Confidence, and Discernment)

iii) Stress Reduction

iv) Studying and knowledge building

2) Afternoon/Mid-Day Meditation

a) Theta Wave Meditation (4Hz| 8Hz)

i) Deep sleep to waking positive thinking

ii) Inspiration/ feeling inspired

iii) Creativity

3) Delta Meditation (0.1 Hz| 4 Hz)

a) To fall asleep

b) Problem solving

c) Pain relief

d) Deep healing

Other frequencies to consider are Beta (13 Hz|30Hz) for focused attention and intentional thinking, and Gamma (30Hz and above) for peak awareness and memory recall. (Source: Healthline.com)

Understanding How the Brain Functions

<u>**Left Side of Brain Brain**</u>   <u>**Right Side of**</u>

Left Side of Brain	Right Side of Brain
Facts & Logic	Emotions & Reactions to Memories
Analyzes Information	Senses and Sensory Information
Organizes Events	Intuition
Speech	PTSD Flashbacks
Blacks out during flashbacks	Imagination
Loss of Executive Functioning	Non-Verbal Cues
Writing	Creativity, Art, Rhythm
Controls right side of body	Controls left side of body
Listening	Face/visual recognition

When Trauma and/or Mood Dysregulation Happens to the Brain

Left Side of Brain

Struggles to understand written & spoken language

Changes in Speech

Verbal memory loss

Impaired logic

Change in art & music creativity

Right Side of Brain

Attention deficit

Memory Issues

Lack of self-awareness

Loss of "big picture" thinking

<u>Care Practices that Improve Brain Functioning</u>

<u>Left Side of Brain</u>	<u>Right Side of Brain</u>
Learning new languages,	Mindful Movement
Word puzzles	Meditation, and Yoga
Sudoku Card Games	
Card Games Aromatherapy	
Puzzles Arts and crafts	
Team Video games 1st person video games	

Bibliography

Afua, Queen (2002). Heal Thyself for Health and Longevity. EWorld Inc., Hunlock Creek, PA.

Ashby, Muata (2005). Glorious Light Meditation: The Oldest Meditation System in History from Ancient Egypt. Sema Institute, Miami, FL.

Brown, Adrienne M. (2019). Pleasure Activism: The Politics of Feeling Good. AK Press. Chico, CA.

Dana, D., & Porges, S. W. (2020). Polyvagal exercises for safety and connection: 50 client-centered practices. W.W. Norton & Company.

Dispenza, Joe. (2017) Becoming Supernatural: How Common People Are Doing the Uncommon. Carlsbad, CA.: Hay House, Inc.

Herman, Judith (2022). Trauma and Recovery: The Aftermath of Violence-From Domestic Violence to Political Terror. Basic Books. New York, NY.

Hersey, Tricia. (2022). Rest is Resistance: A Manifesto—little, Brown Spark Publishing: New York, NY.

Bibliography (continued)

hooks. bell. (2000). All about Love: New Visions. New York: William Morrow

Kudumu, Negarra (2020). Spiritual Hygiene eBook. Crossroads Healing Arts. Seattle, WA.

Lehmiller, J. (2017). The Psychology of Human Sexuality (2nd ed.). Wiley-Blackwell. Thousand Oaks, CA.

Lorde, A. (1984). The Master's Tools Will Never Dismantle the Master's House. In Essays & Speeches by Audre Lorde (pp. 110-113). New York, NY: Random House

Lorde, A. (1984). Uses of the erotic: The Erotic as Power. In Essays & Speeches by Audre Lorde (pp. 53-59). New York, NY: Random House.

Medical News Today. (2023, April 27). *Aromatherapy: Do essential oils really work?* https://www.medicalnewstoday.com/articles/10884#essential_oils

Bibliography (continued)

Moore, Cassie, Jesse Caffyn, and Yahya, Mehdi D. (2017). Healers on the Edge: Somatic Sex Education. erospirt. British Columbia, Canada.

National Institutes of Health Office of Dietary Supplements (2002). White House Commission on Complementary and Alternative Medicine Policy. https://ods.od.nih.gov/HealthInformation/White_House_CAM_Commission.aspx

Page, Cara. Kindred: Southern Healing Justice Collective (2005). Healing Justice.

Page, Cara. Woodland, Erica (2023). Healing Justice Lineages: Dreaming at the Crossroads of Liberation, Collective Care, and Safety. North Atlantic Books. Berkeley, CA.

Peck, M. Scott (1998). The Road Less Traveled: A New Psychology of Love, Traditional Values, and Spiritual Growth. Simon & Schuster. Manhattan, NY.

Peterson, Amina (2022). The Breath & Stillness of Sex: Everyday Intimacy Made Magical. The Amina Institute for Embodiment & Healing. Panama City, Panama.

Bibliography (continued)

Peterson, Amina (2025). Authentic Consent Instructor Training. The Amina Institute for Embodiment & Healing. Panama City, Panama

Queen, Lena (2023). Healing the Erotic Self. TWSHI Publishing. Middletown, DE

Queen, T. L. (2025). Cultivating capacity: Supporting professional capacity, burnout support, and burnout recovery to achieve LGBTQIA+ health equity. *Delaware Journal of Public Health*, *11*(2), 100–117. https://doi.org/10.32481/djph.2025.07.18

Taylor, Sonya R. (2018). The Body is NOT an Apology. Berrett-Koehler Publishers. Oakland, CA.

About the Author

Mx. Lena Queen, LCSW, M.Ed. (Queen/they) is a licensed clinical social worker (DE & NJ) and clinical supervisor, is a multifaceted liberation-centered professional and self-liberator. Mx. Queen is a trauma-informed integrative somatic sex(uality) therapist and sex(uality) educator, erotic hypnotherapist, energy healer, Bliss breathwork facilitator, TEDx Speaker, and professional development consultant and trainer.

 With over 23 years of personal and professional healing experience, they are an embodied and erotic liberation author and creator of the Healing the Erotic Self Erotic Liberation Ecosystem which includes the erotic intelligence workbook and the 6-week erotic embodiment healing intensive, Healing The Erotic

Self (HTES), The Other EQ: Erotic Intelligence Masterclass, in addition to the SHIFT Somatic Healing Book & 3-Day Intensive. Founder of the non-profit erotic healing and learning space, Erospirituality Centre, activating erotic intelligence for embodied liberation while centering Black erotic healing, Mx. Queen uses the erotic to help others create embodied safety and self-trust to heal and create an intuitive, erotically empowered lovership. Mx. Queen is a member of the American Association of Sexuality Educators, Counselors, and Therapists (AASECT) and an AASECT-approved continuing education (CE) provider.

You can discover more about Queen's healing and learning intensives, masterclasses, and erotic living course and erotic liberation resources at Erospirituality.com and SistaSexologist.com.